MW01482701

KR Jul 17

THE
CONSTRUCTED
MENNONITE

THE CONSTRUCTED MENNONITE

History, Memory, and the Second World War

Hans Werner

UMP
University of Manitoba Press

University of Manitoba Press
Winnipeg, Manitoba
Canada R3T 2M5
uofmpress.ca

© Hans Werner 2013

Printed in Canada
Text printed on chlorine-free, 100% post-consumer recycled paper

16 15 14 13   1 2 3 4 5

All rights reserved. No part of this publication may be reproduced or transmitted in
any form or by any means, or stored in a database and retrieval system in Canada,
without the prior written permission of the University of Manitoba Press, or, in the case
of photocopying or any other reprographic copying, a licence from Access Copyright
(Canadian Copyright Licensing Agency). For an Access Copyright licence,
visit www.accesscopyright.ca, or call 1-800-893-5777.

Cover design: Frank Reimer
Interior design: Karen Armstrong Graphic Design
Maps: Weldon Hiebert
All photos courtesy the author.

Library and Archives Canada Cataloguing in Publication

Werner, Hans, 1952–
The constructed Mennonite : history, memory, and the Second
World War / Hans Werner.

Includes bibliographical references and index.
Issued also in electronic formats.
ISBN 978-0-88755-741-5 (pbk.)
ISBN 978-0-88755-436-0 (PDF e-book)
ISBN 978-0-88755-438-4 (epub e-book)

1. Werner, John, 1917–2003. 2. Mennonites—Russia (Federation)—
Siberia—Biography. 3. Mennonites—Manitoba—Biography. 4. Immigrants—
Manitoba—Biography. 5. Storytellers—Manitoba—Biography. 6. Ex-prisoners
of war—Manitoba—Biography. 7. World War, 1939–1945—Biography.
8. World War, 1939-1945—Influence. 9. Autobiographical memory. I. Title.

BX8143.W37W37 2013   289.7092   C2012-908123-X

The University of Manitoba Press gratefully acknowledges the financial
support for its publication program provided by the Government of Canada
through the Canada Book Fund, the Canada Council for the Arts, the Manitoba
Department of Culture, Heritage, Tourism, the Manitoba Arts Council,
and the Manitoba Book Publishing Tax Credit.

FSC
www.fsc.org
MIX
Paper from
responsible sources
FSC® C016245

Contents

To Kadin, Abigail, Anna and David

Acknowledgements

I want to thank Royden Loewen, Dan Stone, Melissa Werner, Jim Suderman and the anonymous readers for U of M Press for taking the time to read and offer thoughtful comments on earlier versions of this book. I am also indebted to archivists at the Mennonite Heritage Centre in Winnipeg, the Mennonite Church Archives at Goshen College, Goshen, Indiana, and the German Military Archives in Freiburg, Germany, for their assistance in helping me to uncover and make available what were often obscure sources. It was a pleasure working with Weldon Hiebert on the maps and I again benefitted from the patience and interest of David Carr and his staff at U of M Press. I am most indebted to my parents, John and Margaret Werner, both of whom have passed on, for patiently telling their stories over and over again. In spite of this much appreciated assistance, the responsibility for what is in these pages is solely mine.

Illustrations

Maps

Photographs

THE
CONSTRUCTED
MENNONITE

Introduction

IT WAS ONE OF THOSE MARCH DAYS in the southern Canadian prairies when the sun's warmth has the feel of spring but the air still has an edge of winter. I travelled alone from Winnipeg to Steinbach, Manitoba, a small city forty-five minutes away where I had grown up, to visit my father in the hospital. He had been diagnosed with stomach cancer some months earlier and had steadily been losing weight because he could no longer eat properly. When the surgeon performed exploratory surgery, it was I who had to tell my father there was nothing that could be done for his illness, and though it was not a subject he discussed, he knew he was dying. On this Sunday, I knew I would be alone with him, and the thought crossed my mind that the circumstances of my visit might free him to tell stories he had never told before.

My father told stories about his life experiences for as long as I can remember, and together with my mother's autobiography his stories of the Stalinist years in the Soviet Union, the experiences of the Second World War, and the immigrant experience in Canada framed who we were and are. The stories were fantastic tales for a boy growing up in a sleepy Mennonite town in southern Manitoba. My need to understand my father's stories became more acute when I became an adult, and in the 1980s, some twenty years before the March trip, I interviewed my parents more formally and tried to uncover any additional sources that could shed light on their remarkable life story.

The primary subject of this book is my father's story and how it was told, and the book has two purposes—the first is to tell the life story of an otherwise ordinary person who experienced the upheavals of the twentieth century in the form of war and totalitarianism from a unique perspective. As David Thelen says in an essay on the relationship between individual experience and history, this account of my father's life is an attempt to join "the process of creating history" with the "experience of living life."[1]

My father was born to Johann and Anna (Janzen) Werner in 1917, just after the Bolshevik Revolution. He was named Hans, and in the German-speaking community where he grew up he kept that name until he went to school. Then in Stalinist Russia he became "Ivan" and part of Stalin's hope to transform the Soviet Union into a strong, industrialized bastion of communism. When war enveloped the world, he fought as a Red Army soldier, first in the Winter War with Finland, then as a junior officer stationed on the German–Soviet frontier when the Nazi armies attacked the Soviet Union in June 1941. A new era would begin for him when he was captured by the Germans, only to be resettled in occupied Poland, where he became "Johann," was naturalized, and then drafted into Hitler's German army. He fought on the Western Front for the rest of the war before being captured by the Americans in April 1945, a month before the war ended. He was a U.S. prisoner of war until 1946, when he was released and began trying to emigrate to Canada. Before that happened, he married my mother, a refugee with many of the same experiences, and after they finally arrived in Canada in 1952 his life in a new country would be marked by another name change. He became "John" and lived the life of an ordinary postwar immigrant finding his way in Canada.

The series of names—Hans, Ivan, Johann, and John—while referring to the same person mark the various ethnic and national identities that my father negotiated. Each name change in my retelling of his story marks a change in who he was. To his children, however, he was always "Papa." His main credits were that he was a skilled auto mechanic, a good husband and provider, the father of a suburban postwar baby boom family. He was always an immigrant in the sense that he never spoke English fluently and was somewhat of an outsider because of his distinctly military past in a town with a sense of itself as a pacifist religious community.

In her reference to Art Spiegelman's *Maus*, the graphic biography of Spiegelman's father, a Holocaust survivor, Susan Engel suggests that the story is "told twice, once to his son and then again to us, his son's readers." It is also heard by two audiences, the "son who is finding out what his father endured and why his father is the way he is," and the "rest of us, hearing the grim details that augment and bleakly enliven what we know about a distant time and place."[2] The stories told here have a similar pattern. My father's stories were told first to private audiences, and with this writing they become public and history. From his memories and stories, we gain another perspective on what Stalinism, Nazism, famine, war, and migration meant. His memories in that sense become part of what the collective memory of these events is and will be.

My second purpose in writing this book is to explore the nature of auto-biographical memory. Scholarship in literature, the neurosciences, and oral history has illustrated the complexity of understanding what we can actually remember about the past, how memory works at the level of the brain, and how we construct the narratives that tell others about what we remember. My father was a good storyteller who captivated many casual listeners with tales of his experiences. I heard him tell stories for forty years or more and have heard many of them repeated innumerable times. Some stories were told sparingly, and occasionally he allowed fleeting glimpses into his memory, exposing details that did not otherwise appear in his stories. Some of his stories had gaps, and he kept secrets that he never told but that other research uncovered.

The stories we tell about our pasts fall into the category of what psychologists call episodic memory, "the kind of memory that allows one to remember past happenings from one's life." It belongs to what has become accepted as long-term memory but is different from semantic memory, the more general knowledge that all of us know and remember, such as how to ride a bicycle.[3] The intricacy of how the brain remembers is beyond the scope of what I can consider here; however, autobiographical memories are not limited to the functions of the brain but are also the domain of narrative and language. We not only remember but also tell, and we can only know about someone's autobiographical past when he or she conveys it to us in language. Psychologist Ulrich Neisser concludes that "the consistency and accuracy of memories is an achievement, not a mechanical production. Stories have a life of their own."[4] The stories my father told had a life of their own, and the following pages are also about the way he told them. We are always constructing ourselves when we share memories of our past lives with others. My father's stories are a part of creating the self, using "autobiographical material as a way to know and communicate who we are now."[5]

Writing about one's father is hardly an exercise embarked on from some distant vantage point or objective hilltop. My father's story is also my story. My interest in history was stimulated to a large extent by my attempts to come to terms with, contextualize, and make sense of my father's many stories. Jill Ker Conway's question of "what we can make of...the network of kin who constitute our tribal past" has a necessarily personal answer: "if we can know them, they are a set of compass points by which we can chart our own course." In her case, discovering that her father's early death could be explained by the same heart condition she had "changed the emotional and moral climate" of her childhood and offered "personal evidence of how much history matters."[6] For me, the history of the Second World War was always framed in terms of my father's experience, and to a large extent my quest to understand his story drew me into more formal studies of history.

Not surprisingly the main sources for this book are my father's stories, told to visitors in our home, sometimes to us as children, and then formally in interviews I conducted with my father in the mid-1980s when he was in his sixties. My interviews were not informed by any reflection on oral history methodology. They were also quite different from what might be termed an "oral history project" in the sense that I, as interviewer, was the son of the subject and both benefited from and was constrained by my own memories of stories my father had told ever since I was old enough to remember them. The interviews were conducted in the Low German language, in which he was most comfortable, then transcribed and translated. The interviews were interspersed with research in secondary and some significant primary sources, which then became parts of annotations to the original transcriptions. The later interviews revisited some of the stories told earlier and were tempered by my deepened understanding of the contexts of the stories. Although I seldom made direct reference to additional research, the later interviews attempted to resolve gaps and inconsistencies in his stories more specifically. Some of what I uncovered in additional research, however, was never raised in subsequent interviews. After the formal interviews, I had occasional conversations with my father that revisited some of his stories more informally. Only notes were kept of these interactions.

There are significant additional primary sources that inform this book. My father kept a limited number of personal documents from the postwar period in Germany. They included a German driver's licence, various work-related documents, and a document pertaining to his release as a prisoner of war. The Mennonite Church Archives in Goshen, Indiana, are the repository of the records of the Mennonite Central Committee and are home to the records of its work with refugees in postwar Germany. These records proved invaluable for reconstructing the process of my father's immigration to Canada. The files of the Berlin Documents Centre, since transferred back to Germany, contained the records of his naturalization as a German citizen in the 1940s. In the German Military Archives in Freiburg, a valuable collection of war diaries pertaining to his unit turned up, and the Deutsche Dienstelle, a German government organization dedicated to maintaining the records of former members of the German military, was invaluable in providing the details of my father's military service. A memoir written by his aunt became available some time after I interviewed my father in the 1980s, and it told the story of the Werner family before my father's birth. The memoir was brought by family members from the Soviet Union who immigrated to Germany after the fall of the Berlin Wall in 1989, an event that signalled the beginning of the collapse of communism and finally permitted ethnic Germans to emigrate in large numbers.[7]

Although the focus here is primarily on my father, Chapter 11 contrasts many of his memories with those of my mother, who experienced the same historical events but from the point of view of a woman, not a soldier. Her story relies on many of the same sources, and my interviews with her were conducted in the same time period as those with my father. The memories of my father's aunt and those of my mother suggest gendered points of divergence in the telling of life stories.

The contexts of the lives recounted here transcend a number of national, ethnic, and linguistic boundaries. The webs of autobiographical memories explored in these pages are inexorably entwined with the primary relationships of family, and the contexts of revolution, war, and migration contribute to complex familial relationships in my family's stories. To help the reader navigate these webs, there are maps and photos interspersed in the text, an appendix with family trees for both my parents, and a glossary of terms and foreign words that appear in the stories.

When I visited my father in the hospital on that March Sunday in 2003, I came away without any new stories. The stories that had been untold remained untold. A short while later he died, and his autobiographical memory took on a new form as the memory of a father's stories told and retold, giving him a form of immortality.

PART I

Siberia

Beginnings

MY FATHER TOLD MANY STORIES, and, like most children, I developed an interest at some point in knowing more about my grandparents and great-grandparents. When I asked him about earlier Werner family history, he remembered almost nothing. He could tell me he was born in Russia in 1917 in the village of Nikolaipol on the West Siberian plain just after the Russian Revolution, an event that would change the world for his and many other families. His name, Hans Werner, made it clear he was not Slavic. The turmoil that enveloped families in Russia around the time he was born and for many years thereafter had seemingly destroyed the desire of his family to narrate or for him to absorb the past before his birth in any significant way. In the stories he told, only fragments of memory shed light on anything of the family's history before his birth. His mother's family name was Janzen, a common name among Mennonites in Russia, and he thought he remembered her telling him they had migrated to Siberia from Zagradovka, a Mennonite colony in Ukraine.

Mennonites trace their origins to the radical wing of Luther's Protestant Reformation of the sixteenth century. These radical reformers believed that Luther had not gone far enough, particularly on the question of membership in the church. In their understanding, only adult believers should be baptized and become members of the church. As a result, they were rebaptized and came to be known as Anabaptists. They also developed a distinctive belief that the Christian should be a pacifist. The persecution that came their way because of what were considered heretical beliefs helped to create a sectarian view of Christianity manifested in a desire to live apart from others—whom they considered part of "the world." To secure freedom to practise their radical beliefs, Anabaptists negotiated with various rulers who granted them military exemption and other privileges in exchange for their promise to be productive and orderly subjects. In the sixteenth and seventeenth centuries, the Dutch–North German branch of these Anabaptists came to be known as Mennonites after Menno Simons, one of their early Dutch leaders. At the same time, some of them migrated to settle the lowlands of the Vistula Delta in West Prussia. In the late eighteenth century and early nineteenth century, two waves of Mennonites from the Vistula Delta accepted an invitation from Catherine the Great to peasants all over Europe to settle the lands she had recently conquered in her wars with the Turks.

Mennonites from Prussia established two major colonies in Catherine's New Russia, now Ukraine. The Old Colony, as it became known, was founded in 1789 at the junction of the Chortitza and Dnieper Rivers in the later province of Ekaterinoslav. The second colony was established a few years later along the Molotschna River in the province of Taurida. The tsarina's hope, and that of her successors, was that Mennonites would be model farmers for their peasant subjects, but there was also a desire among both tsars and Mennonites for them to live separately from their Russian neighbours. By the First World War, Mennonites had established a commonwealth of colonies and daughter colonies across the tsar's empire. The colony of Zagradovka of my father's memory was one of them.

The earliest Mennonites to establish themselves in far-off Siberia were wealthy landowners who purchased large tracts of land from the Cossacks and in some cases established enterprises such as mills and farm equipment dealerships. Although the wealthiest Mennonites in Russia owned large estates or industrial enterprises, Mennonites generally had become wealthy relative to their Slavic peasant neighbours. They had developed numerous institutions and a distinctive Russian Mennonite culture that used a particular dialect of Low German in daily exchange and gradually High German for church, business, and other formal communication.

My father was not sure but thought his parents had married in Siberia. His father died in a cholera epidemic when he was only four years old, and the connection with the extended Werner family was broken at that point. He had vague recollections of being told his grandfather had lived in Russia "on a German passport," but it was not entirely clear what that meant. Did it mean he had never become a Russian citizen or only that he had been born in Germany? It often seemed my father preferred to believe the Werners had not been Mennonite but were of Black Sea German colonist stock. Lutheran and Catholic Germans had also accepted Catherine's invitation and settled in colonies north of the Black Sea in Ukraine, not far from the Mennonite colonies. They were called colonists to distinguish them from their German-speaking Mennonite counterparts.

One story my father enjoyed telling did shed some light on earlier Werner family history. Sometime in the 1930s he and a group of other young people managed to get permission to use a truck from their collective farm to take a trip to the area where the Werner family had lived when he was a child. My father remembered paying his aunt, Tina (Werner) Hinz, a visit. Some of the Siberian villages had both a number and a name, and the Hinzes lived in a village that was one of a cluster of small settlements known as the "Eighties Villages." After visiting his aunt, my father travelled farther to Nikolaipol to visit his grandmother. During the visit, she told him to guard the Werner name because he was the only surviving male member of the family. According to her, all the others had died at the same time as his father. He remembered little else of the visit with her other than she had been a small, wiry woman.

The mist of the past had seemingly enveloped everything else about where the Werner family had originated. It left many questions. Although it seemed that with a name like Janzen my grandmother's family was certainly Mennonite, whether the Werners were Mennonite remained unclear.

When I became interested in discovering more about the Werner family origins, I did come across rare occurrences of the name Werner in Mennonite genealogical records. That at least left open the possibility that the Werner family was Mennonite. I chased down other hints—a possible relative who had moved to Brazil; a Mennonite pastor who had officiated at my parents' wedding, spent time in Siberia, and apparently come across a Werner family there; and genealogical records of Black Sea Germans. Nothing seemed to offer any hope of uncovering a Werner past that connected to my father. It seemed I would have to be content with him just having "appeared" on the Siberian plain in 1917.

The cholera epidemic that took the lives of most of the male members of the Werner family struck the village of Nikolaipol in the summer of 1921

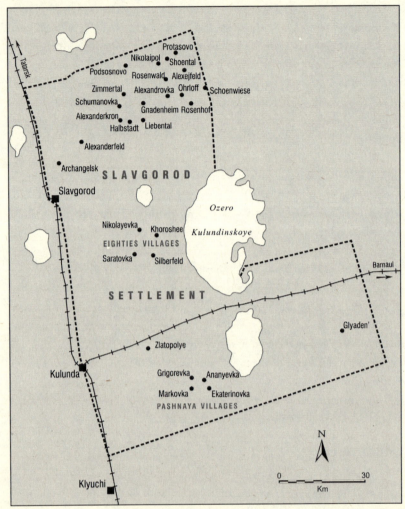

Map 1. Mennonite settlements on the Kunlunda Steppe.

and resulted in the quarantine of the village until the fall, when it was believed that the cooler temperatures would reduce the potency of the disease.
When movement into and out of the village resumed, the reality of how my
grandmother, Anna (Janzen) Werner, and her family were to survive hit
home. It seems she had few options other than depending on the goodwill of
her brothers Aaron and Julius Janzen. Both lived in the village of Silberfeld,[1]
another of the Eighties Villages located about fifty kilometres southeast of
Nikolaipol. In late fall 1921, Aaron came to get his sister and her family. Life

in the Soviet Union of the 1920s was not easy, and it seems Anna's brothers struggled with their own families, adding even more impetus to the need for Anna to remarry quickly. It is unclear how the unfortunate choice of a husband was made, but she married a German colonist with a last name my father remembered only as Jon or Jonas. He thought he was from village number eighty-five; however, if his recollection that the village was the same one where his aunt Tina (Werner) Hinz lived sometime later is accurate, it would have been Khoroshee, a neighbouring village to Silberfeld, the home of the Aaron Janzens.[2] Khoroshee was village number eighty-seven, and Jonas lived there with one daughter who was approximately Hans's age and a deaf mute. Only young Hans became part of the family created by the new marriage; his sisters Sara and Aganetha remained with their Janzen uncles, Sara with Julius, Aganetha with Aaron. It is also unclear exactly when the marriage to Jonas took place, but it was likely in February 1923.

My father did recall that Jonas made *samohonka*, or moonshine, and was an alcoholic. He was always drunk and frequently abusive. Young Hans was often physically abused, particularly when the two children did not play well together—a frequent occurrence aggravated by his stepsister's disability. Although my father had a general recollection of these days, his memories were fragmented. His stories never conveyed any sense of how seriously he had been abused; he never mentioned specific injuries or incidents. My father stuttered, and some explanations suggest that stress during the time when a child is learning to talk can aggravate, or even contribute to, stuttering. Perhaps his stuttering originated in part from the abuses suffered at the hands of his stepfather.[3] The unfortunate marriage to Jonas quickly became unbearable for Anna, and by May or June 1923 Hans ran away, or, as he corrected himself, his mother sent the six-year-old boy back to the Janzens in Silberfeld. It was not that far away, and he knew the way because he had walked there often with his mother. The Janzen brothers sent someone on horseback to let his mother know that he had arrived safely, and some time thereafter came to take her out of what was obviously an unbearable situation, one in which she was likely also being abused. Anna returned to the Aaron Janzens, but she had become pregnant. My father recalled how during the night his uncle Aaron had rolled him up in a blanket and carried him to the home of his other uncle, Jacob Janzen. When he woke up, he wanted to go back, but his older sister Sara, also there, suggested he stay with them for a few days. Tina, or Katya as she would be called, was born on 8 February 1924, and, while the Werner children kept the Werner family name after the marriage to Jonas, Katya was apparently not given the name of her father. The memories of the marriage to Jonas did not fit with the narrative the family wanted to sustain, and my visits with Katya many years later added nothing further to the story.

With the separation from Jonas, the need for a husband to help provide a stable economic basis for her family became a pressing issue again, and Anna soon remarried a second time. It is unclear how the marriage to Jonas was formally ended, though it seems he soon died as a result of his excessive drinking, and there might not have been a need for a formal divorce. In March 1924, a month after Tina was born, Anna married Johann Froese, a widower from Pashnaya, a group of villages located some forty or fifty kilometres south of Silberfeld. Her remarriage meant further separation for the remnants of the Johann and Anna (Janzen) Werner family. My father remembered being packed up in a sleigh for the journey to Grigorevka, where Froese farmed. His new stepfather had a family from his first marriage, and my father remembered being greeted warmly when they arrived. Again only young Hans and the infant Katya became a permanent part of the new family. Sara spent considerable time at the Julius Janzens, while Aganetha seems not to have joined the Froese family at all. Froese's family included another younger Sara, called "Little Sara" to distinguish her from "Big Sara" Werner. There were also boys, Herman and Johann, and another daughter, Maria. The marriage to Johann Froese finally brought some stability to the remnants of the Johann Werner family. Improving economic prospects for the peasants on the Siberian steppe helped it along. By the spring of 1924, when Anna remarried, the Soviet regime had stepped back from the harsh economic restrictions of the civil war years. The New Economic Policy or NEP period was implemented in 1921 while Lenin was still alive, and it allowed considerable free-market activities for peasants and a slight relaxation of social and religious restrictions. Peasant farmers such as the Froese family were able to sell their grain and gain some measure of economic stability, though basic consumer goods remained unavailable.

The Kulunda Steppe, the area in which Grigorevka and the other Mennonite settlements were located, is a vast and austere landscape. When I visited the Slavgorod area in 2010, it reminded me of the Canadian prairies. The landscape was as flat and treeless as parts of the Red River Valley and dotted with salt lakes like southwestern Saskatchewan. The West Siberian plain was still a wild frontier in the 1920s, at least in the eyes of a European

The outlines of the former village street of the village of Grigorevka in the foreground leave but a small imprint on the vast Kulunda Steppe. Photo by the author, 2010.

traveller. In his writings, Helmut Anger, a German academic travelling in Siberia in the fall of 1926, noted the conversations he had with fellow travellers about the presence of wolves, confirmed by the remains of animals that he saw from the horse-drawn carriages on which he travelled. Among the few stories my father could tell about my grandfather was one about wolves. When his father, Johann Werner, had gone to see the neighbours on a winter evening, his mother heard a hurried knock on the window and made out the shadow of her husband, who immediately disappeared only to knock again on another window. She went to the door to undo the latch, and he burst in and quickly closed the door behind him. He was out of breath because a wolf had been following him.

Anger had some difficulties hiring drivers to take him around the countryside. He noted particularly the hesitancy of sceptical Mennonite farmers he approached to hire to take him to the next village. He was clearly an outsider, and he attributed their reluctance to previous negative experiences with curious visitors from Germany. On his way to Grigorevka, the village where Hans was a young boy at the time, they passed by one of the numerous salt lakes that dotted the plain, and he painted a picture typical of the Kulunda Steppe. The lake was "surrounded by the brown steppe along whose shore some kind of salt loving weeds formed a red carpet and whose surface mirrored the blue sky and some large dark, but golden rimmed clouds." Anger described the four Pashnaya villages, of which Grigorevka was one, as "poorer than any of the other Mennonite villages I saw on my trip." His hosts pointed to poorer soils as the cause, with wheat averaging twelve bushels per acre compared with the twenty to twenty-five that could be obtained in the Omsk region. In Grigorevka, Anger stayed with the village mayor, whose home he characterized as "poor, but clean." In the evening, his host's yard was filled with young males who played a game that, from his description, sounded a lot like dodge ball. My father, nine at the time, was probably too young to have participated. Based on Anger's one day of interaction with the villagers, life in Grigorevka was difficult but stable economically and socially.[4]

Although life in his new home seemed to offer promise, my father's memories of growing up in the Froese household were not pleasant. Johann Froese was a troubled man with a vicious temper. He often took his anger out on his young stepson, and his own sons often had to rescue the youngster to prevent serious physical harm. My father recalled a windy harvest scene in which it was his job to climb on a load of sheaves to trample them down so that the wind would not blow them off the wagon. The wind kept catching the sheaves before he could get to them, and his stepfather, in a fit of rage, thrust the pitchfork at him, shrieking that he would "spear all the holy ones." Herman and Johann quickly had to help young Hans down the back of the wagon, and he scurried to safety while Froese continued to thrust his pitchfork in the direction where the young lad had just been. Hans suffered other humiliations. It was common in winter for household members to relieve themselves in the barn. Young Hans was not allowed to use the gutter in the barn, like the rest of the family did, and had to go in his own special area.

His memories of childhood were not all bad. Hans had fond memories of visiting the Aaron Janzen home and playing with his cousins, Sara and Aaron. On one occasion, they were playing blind man's bluff in a room lit by a kerosene lamp with a round burner and large shade that hung from the ceiling. While dashing around the room, one of the children jumped up on the table, hitting her head on the lamp. The lamp came crashing down, but fortunately his older sister Sara put the fire out before the house burned down. They were all in trouble with their parents, and a severe scolding resulted. Another family story told with a certain fondness made light of the extreme shortages of clothing that plagued Siberian families in the 1920s. Since Hans was the only young boy in the family, and with a stepsister close to his age, he had worn only dresses before going to school. When he received his first pair of pants, he cried, not wanting to wear them for his first day of school.

As a boy, Hans also spent time with his Janzen relatives. One summer his uncle Jacob requested that he come to stay at their home for the summer. Grandmother Janzen was ill, and because the rest of the Janzen family were heavy sleepers the elderly woman could call for help at night until she was hoarse, without being heard. Hans was a light sleeper, so he spent the summer at his uncle's house, getting up at night when his grandmother knocked on the wall of his adjoining room. He would bring her a glass of water or whatever else she needed. During the day, he helped with chores on the farm.

School was in the village schoolhouse in Grigorevka and was conducted in both German and Russian before 1929 and only in Russian thereafter. The teacher, Mr. Derksen, could draw well and used his gift to illustrate the "letter of the day" by drawing an animal or bird that reminded his charges of the letter with which its name began. The children sat in rows, with the youngest at the front. Students were promoted each year, and when they were in the highest grade they sat at the back of the room. The turmoil of the revolution and civil war disrupted Mennonite education severely. Teachers were paid poorly, if at all, and though my father recalled the school had six grades the questionnaires he filled out some fifteen years later in Germany indicated he had only four years of formal schooling.[5] He would always be hindered by the inability to read and write beyond a basic level in either German or Russian.

The village was the centre of social and, to the extent possible, religious life. The Loewens living beside the Froeses, the Martens across the street, the Rogalskys a little farther down the street—these became the families from which friends and marriage partners would be chosen and with whom the Froese family would socialize. Young Hans soon had close friends among the boys from the village who were his age: Jacob Wiebe, Abram Martens, and Henry Matthies. Religion was an even less formal part of his life. Hans remembered there had been Mennonite ministers but recalled little else about religious life. He recalled one occasion when he attended a baptism. He visualized it being on the riverbank, indicating that the baptism of the candidate was by total immersion, a practice of the Mennonite Brethren Church. The Mennonite Brethren had separated from the main, or Kirchliche Mennonite Church, in the 1860s in Ukraine. Although maintaining a Mennonite religious identity that included adult baptism, they were distinguished by their insistence on baptism by complete immersion as opposed to the pouring or sprinkling of water on the head, as practised by the Kirchliche. Hans thought his mother was Mennonite Brethren but had become part of the main Kirchliche group when she married Froese. Surviving letters sent to Canada bear out that Anna (Janzen) Werner was a woman of faith, but religious life seems not to have been an important part of my father's early years.

Few of us remember anything before our fourth birthday. Childhood amnesia is a perplexing aspect of human memory. Although a three-year-old's memory is astoundingly sharp, it is either inaccessible or lost after the child reaches about four years of age. The cholera epidemic that wiped out much of the Werner family occurred when my father was three years and eight months old, and he had no direct recollection of these events even though they would have been traumatic and memorable. It seems we have no long-term memories until we have acquired a certain level of language. Geoffrey Cubitt notes that we learn how to remember from adults, who assist our "participation in conversations." Our parents foster our early memories and provide "most of the structure and…initial content of the narrative" we are "encouraged to form and regard as…our own."[6] What is known about the consequences of the deaths of my grandfather and the rest of the men in the Werner family is mostly conjecture and a few fragments of what my father remembered being told. Perhaps there was no context in which my grandmother felt safe enough to provide the narrative structures that would have allowed the young boy to acquire memories of his father's and grandfather's lives and deaths. Although my father's early years were troubled, the challenges presented by the death of his father and remarriages of his mother were mostly borne by her and really did not influence or form significant memories for my father. Children are resilient, and though his stuttering might have been stimulated or aggravated by the abuse suffered at the hands of his first stepfather he would survive much more than he could have imagined. The difficult years were not behind him, and as he grew up he would have many more vivid memories of difficult times.

Difficult Years

My FATHER RARELY TOLD STORIES that offered a window into his mother's difficult life. One story, together with surviving fragments of letters from his mother, offers such a window. Sometime in 1925 Aaron Janzen decided suddenly to emigrate to Canada. Mennonites from Ukraine had been actively seeking ways to leave the Soviet Union ever since the Bolsheviks had gained control of the country during the civil war. In the early 1920s, this finally became possible, but relatively few families from Siberia availed themselves of this tenuous opportunity to escape. Although emigration fever also gripped the Mennonites in Siberia after the revolution, it seems the NEP period tempered this desire to the extent that the complications of emigration from Siberia were enough to result in few actual migrants. Historian Manfred Klaube notes that only thirty-seven families from the Slavgorod region left for Canada between 1920 and 1928.[1]

Exactly why Aaron decided to leave Siberia so quickly was the subject of some speculation among the family members who stayed behind, but because of the circumstances my grandmother tended to believe the worst. Aaron had the nickname "Trader Janzen"[2] because he was a horse trader during the NEP years, and it was believed a deal had gone sour, so emigrating was a way of escaping the consequences. In any event, when the Aaron Janzen family emigrated to Canada, they took Aganetha with them. According to immigration records, the family left Slavgorod in October 1925 to settle in Steinbach, Manitoba. The record of the Canadian Mennonite Board of Colonization, the agency created by Canadian Mennonites to assist immigration, simply lists Aganetha as one of the Janzen children. A later note in the record clarifies that she was actually Aganetha Werner.[3]

The stories the various actors told to explain these events bear the marks of their desire to reconcile their own autobiographies with what seems to have been a tragic and deplorable action by Aaron. A number of aspects of the story are consistent in the various accounts. Several sources agree he consulted with Aganetha, painted a glowing picture for her of what awaited them in Canada, and gained her consent. My grandmother's letters to her daughter seem to substantiate that Aaron allowed Aganetha to choose. Anna wrote, "It appears that you are a child who has a mother with a stone heart, that I allowed you to go along. I wrote letters to you in [village] Eighty-Six, to you and Sara. You went along, and Sara stayed here. The flowers that Uncle Aaron painted for you must have often become bitter. Not everything that glitters will be gold there either."[4]

My father's sister Martha, born after these events, also suggests that her "uncle promised" Aganetha "a lot, until she finally agreed."[5] Aganetha's 1989 obituary notes the strong bond that must have developed between her and the Aaron Janzen family that resulted in her making the "difficult decision in 1925 to emigrate with them to Canada."[6] In the one conversation on the subject I was able to have with Aganetha, by then in her seventies, she suggested that, as an eleven-year-old girl who had lived with the Aaron Janzen family for five years, sometimes together with her mother but often by herself, and who was unsure whether she would ever rejoin her family, the decision to emigrate with the Janzen family seemed the only reasonable one.

Regardless of how much justification for Aaron's actions one might allow given the young girl's consent, that Aaron did not obtain consent from her mother created lifelong pain for her and animosity and conflict between her and him. In her first letter to Aganetha, Anna wrote, "I will not forget my entire life what Aaron Janzen did, that he stole my child from me." To aggravate the already difficult circumstances, when Aaron arrived in Canada he sent eleven-year-old Aganetha to work for a Steinbach family as a nanny and maid. In this letter, Anna wondered why Aganetha needed to work for wages. Aaron "took you along—for what? That is not clear to me. There are places here where you can also serve, to work as a babysitter. Is Uncle Aaron so poor that he cannot keep you? Does he not have enough to eat?"[7] The Isaac F. Loewen family, who had hired Aganetha, gradually became aware that she was not Aaron's daughter, and subsequent correspondence from Anna often went to the Loewens. Often a note for Aganetha was enclosed with these letters. In one of these notes, Anna suggests that, "even if you are called Loewen in school, the name Janzen you should not use, or you will be unhappy your entire life."[8] In my father's recollection of these events, his mother was so upset at her brother Aaron that she eventually found a way to prevent him from collecting Aganetha's earnings. Although it is hard to imagine that a Soviet document would have much influence in Canada, my father recalled the occasion when his mother went to the *selsoviet*, the Soviet local government office, to draw up documents that she signed and sealed with a wax seal that officially made the Loewens the guardians of Aganetha, ostensibly eliminating the possibility of Aaron collecting her wages.

For Anna, the relatively easier years that had coincided with her marriage to Johann Froese suddenly came to an end in 1928. That year Stalin, having outmanoeuvred his opponents, made a trip to Siberia, where he berated local authorities over slow grain acquisitions from the countryside. His visit also signalled the beginning of the forced collectivization and dekulakization campaign that would brutalize Soviet peasants of all ethnic origins but be particularly devastating for the peasants of the Kulunda Steppe. Collectivization meant that individual peasants were forced to give up all their land, cattle, and horses. The assets of an entire village were combined into one large collective farm known as a *kolkhoz*, and the former owners became the collective farm's workers. In the process, a campaign ensued designed to root out opposition to collectivization specifically and the regime generally. Being branded a kulak meant the entire family was disenfranchised and resettled, often to nearby villages but occasionally to remote areas.

Forced collectivization began in earnest in the spring of 1929, but the Froese family was ready to leave the Soviet Union by the fall of 1928, when the forced collection of grain began. The repressive measures distressed Johann Froese, and soon he began to speak of nothing else but emigration. His wife's longing to be reunited with her daughter matched and reinforced his dissatisfaction and united the family in their desire to leave everything and go to Canada. The panic that gripped the Froeses assisted their belief in even the wildest rumours of the possibility of escape. In a confusing note to her daughter in 1928, Anna wrote in glowing terms about possible emigration to Paraguay. In her mind, Paraguay bordered on Canada, and she claimed it would become home to a "large settlement. Many people can move there.

Fruit, lemons, oranges, etc., grow there.... Freedom from military duty and school instruction in the German language."[9] By February 1929, the focus had shifted to emigration to Canada, and she informed the Loewens in Steinbach about the costs of such an undertaking: "You might ask how much it would cost for us to cross the ocean, you may find it to be expensive, but there is no harm in writing it. There are five of us that need passports. And a passport costs twenty-five rubles, and then another two, that is, Hans and Sara, the small Sara; they were eleven years old in January. They will need half as much. We have two Saras. Travelling without fare, or on a 'free' card, that is not possible.... However, I still do not know if some will move in spring."[10]

In German villages all over Siberia, similar stirrings signalled an attempt to leave in spite of no assurance from anyone in government that permission to leave would be granted nor indications from a possible receiving country that entry would be permitted. By midsummer of 1929, the desire to leave Siberia was transformed into action when word came that a group of seventy persons, who had left for Moscow while others had only been thinking about it, had been given permission to leave. This news coincided with escalating use of force by the regime to bring about collectivization, particularly in Siberia.[11]

Sometime in the summer of 1929, the Froese family and five or six other families from their village joined the mass flight of German, primarily Mennonite, peasants to Moscow. My father remembered a lot of travelling around by his parents to gather information and discuss plans. Finally it was time to make their move. They tried to sell as much as they could, and my father remembered a well-attended auction sale at which most of the household furnishings, the farm equipment, and the livestock were sold. His job was to catch the chickens so that they could be auctioned. The house, livestock feed, firewood, and some of the land were left to the oldest Froese boy to sell after they left. He was in love with a girl from a family not planning to emigrate, so he planned to stay. The auction sale caused a lot of excitement in the village because, in my father's words, "everything was sold, and we were moving to America."[12] The family packed their clothes and seven bags of roasted *zwieback* (buns), the staple of Mennonite migrations, and boarded the train for Moscow. The train stations along the route were choked with people, and in Tatarsk young Hans was lifted into the train car through a window. The train had four berths per car with a long hallway along one side, and my father remembered the cars being very dirty. It took two days to reach the Ural

A photograph of the Werner-Froese family taken in Moscow in 1929 and referred to as a passport photo. Standing in the back are 'Big' Sara Werner and Herman Froese. Seated are Johann Froese and Anna (Werner) Froese with 'Little' Sara Froese to the left of Anna and my father Hans between Anna and Johann. Katya (Jonas) is the little girl in the front.

Mountains. He recalled they spent three months in the city, indicating they arrived there in late August or early September.

The Froese family lived in the *dachas* on the edges of Moscow, the summer homes of Moscow residents. Their temporary home was in a village near the Perlovka train station, one of Moscow's suburbs. The family seems to have been fortunate enough to obtain ration cards enabling them to buy bread—even if at exorbitant prices. The roasted buns were saved for the trip across the ocean. They were soon joined by swelling numbers of Mennonites and then other German peasants. A report of 18 September 1929 indicated there were 250 families in the areas surrounding Moscow.[13] By 11 October, Otto Auhagen, an expert on Germans in the east who was in Moscow, noted there were 800 Mennonite families totalling 4,500 "souls" on the edges of Moscow. In addition, there were some 100 Lutheran and Catholic families. By 26 October, the number of Mennonite families had risen to 1,030, and the number of Lutheran and Catholic families had doubled, with more arriving every day.[14] It is estimated that in total some 18,000 Germans congregated in Moscow in the fall of 1929.[15]

A preoccupation of the refugees was obtaining the necessary passports for emigration. By late October, the Soviet regime had increased the cost of obtaining passports to 200 rubles, with an additional twenty rubles for the Red Cross. In a letter describing their experience, Anna noted they paid 220 rubles for passports, a much larger amount than the twenty-five rubles she had anticipated in her letter of February 1929.[16]

The flight to Moscow touched off an international incident involving Germany, Canada, and the Soviet Union. The arrival in Moscow of thousands of German peasants determined to flee the Soviet paradise made news around the world. It forced difficult choices on all the governments involved, none of which, sadly, had any real concern for the human tragedy unfolding, even though their officials were strident in their efforts to find a solution to the international incident it was creating. The Soviet Union was caught off guard by the sudden arrival of refugees and the immediate press reaction to their plight. It was afraid of being isolated diplomatically, and relations with Germany factored importantly in its reluctance to take hurried or drastic measures. Germans had the most sympathy for the plight of the refugees from an ethnic and national point of view and offered to provide them with German passports to facilitate their entry to another country as German citizens. Germany, however, could not see its way to actually allowing them to stay in that country because of budget considerations. Canada, the preferred destination, was in the throes of an election campaign, and its evolving approach to immigration policy required greater consultation with the provinces. Saskatchewan's J.T.M. Anderson, an earlier critic of Mennonite separateness, was the most intransigent of the premiers who resisted the enticements Mackenzie King's government was prepared to offer to facilitate further Mennonite immigration.[17] All of this, however, was not part of most of the refugees' knowledge or understanding.

On 19 October 1929, it appeared that the diplomatic negotiations between the various governments would be successful, and the Soviet government promised that all the refugees would be given permission to leave. They were organized into eleven groups, and preparations were made to entrain them. During the night of 27 October, the first train headed for Leningrad, the former St. Petersburg and Petrograd, and the border. On 30 October, news arrived that Canada was reluctant to accept any immigrants but might accept some in the spring if they had jobs. A second train already loaded with refugees was shunted to a siding, and the promise of escape came to an end.[18]

An intense period of negotiation between Germany and Canada, between Canada's federal government and the provinces, and between Canadian Mennonites and the federal government ensued. For a three-week period, negotiations went on while refugees in Moscow waited and hoped without any knowledge of what was really happening. Canadian public opinion was increasingly opposed to admitting any more Eastern Europeans, and Canada would finally indicate formally on 26 November that further negotiations to allow admission of the Mennonites in Moscow would have to wait until the spring. By then, it was too late. In Germany, the tide of public opinion went the other way, but the various state organs could not agree on a plan of action. Finally, on 18 November, the German cabinet authorized funding for the rescue effort without approval of the Budgetary Committee of the German Reichstag. That decision also came too late as the Soviet regime's patience had run out the previous evening. On the evening of 17 November, deportations of the German colonists back to Siberia began.[19]

The Froese family would not make it out of the Soviet Union. Back at home in the village of Grigorevka, Anna reported the sad news to her daughter in Canada.

> We have been sent back. Everything was ready; we just had to board and travel to Leningrad. In the evening, it looked promising; we prepared so that if we got word during the night to go to the station—to wait for good news. Then it was completely different. During the same night, a vehicle came, we boarded, and went back to the railway. The children were happy; we were going to America. I told them right away that we were going back; otherwise, they would not have come to get us. The first and second groups had to provide their own way to the station. After all, it was only three *verst*. I would have willingly, as difficult as it was, gone to the station by myself. That which we wanted to take along, bedding; we would have carried that. The two groups left at night.[20]

Her despair would have deepened had she known what transpired in Moscow a few days after they were sent back. Amid an outburst of diplomatic indignation by the German government, the Soviet regime relented and stopped the deportations on 25 November. There were still approximately 5,600 refugees left in the city, and all were allowed to emigrate. The German government granted them entry, while Mennonite agencies organized their resettlement in Brazil and Paraguay, where they created the Fernheim Colony. Quietly and without fanfare, approximately 1,300 joined their close relatives in Canada.[21]

But for young Hans and his family, the knock on the door and the trucks waiting outside to pick them up signalled the beginning of difficult times. Soldiers came to load the Froese family and other refugees onto the red train cars used to haul cattle. They were crowded together in dark and poorly heated railway cars, forty-two people per car. With the onset of winter, temperatures had begun to fall. People frantically tried to take along as many of their belongings as possible because they knew they would desperately need them. It took twelve days to reach Kulunda, the train station nearest to the village of Grigorevka. For Anna, it was particularly difficult because she was two months shy of her forty-fifth birthday and eight months pregnant. It is hard to imagine what the trip back must have been like for her. They set out for home from Kulunda by sleigh but were soon caught in a terrible snowstorm. They had to stop for the night in the Russian village of Zlatopolye, where a Russian family took them in. That night Anna gave birth to a daughter, whom they named Martha. Johann Froese and Anna with her new baby remained in Zlatopolye for a week, and the other children were taken to the "poor old homestead."[22] My father remembered it took three days to warm up the house. They took turns staying up to feed the central brick oven with straw until the house had sealed itself and retained the heat. Froese's son Johann had managed to sell more of their belongings while they were away, but the money had been placed in the *selsoviet* to be forwarded to them in Moscow. Anna's cryptic reference in a letter to her daughter in Canada that "when we came back the money was still in the soviet, but you can imagine," suggested they never got it back. She went on: "There was a lot of stealing, poor nourishment, no cooking utensils, the house was empty. I wanted to have a little cloth to wrap the child, but there wasn't enough." They had no beds and had to sleep on the straw they had spread on the floor.[23]

Johann Froese, normally a hard worker, became despondent and talked about nothing else than his conviction that he would be arrested. He was sure the Moscow adventure would doom him. On a February evening, an engagement celebration was held at their home, the traditional Mennonite *polta* evening, for a couple from the village. In my father's memory, toward evening Froese said that he was going out to visit, that preparations in the house were too loud for him. This was not uncommon since he often went visiting to "Old" Matthies or the Wiebes across the street. The engagement party went on into the evening without him until the guests all went home. It got to be midnight and then one o'clock in the morning, and Froese had still not returned. Herman, one of the Froese boys, was dating one of the Wiebe girls, and together with my father, who was thirteen, they set out to find his stepfather. They walked down the street to the end of the village where Matthies lived, and there they came upon a single set of footprints in the snow leading to the village herdsman's shack. Mennonite villages were laid out with a community pasture at the end of the village where the herdsman, often a Russian, would tend the villagers' cattle in the summertime. In February, it was empty. Since there was still light in Matthies's window, the two of them decided to ask Matthies to join them. My father continued:

> We went there, and the door was snowed under, and there was one deep footprint leading inside—the door opened to the inside. The door was pushed shut, and snow had come in between so you couldn't close it completely. I had the lantern, and I stooped in and looked. The herdsman's shack was only a small building, a small barn for one horse, at the end a small granary, and then there were two rooms where people could sleep—it was only equipped for the summer. The entire house was empty—and now for the granary—there the door was closed. Herman pushed it, and it opened, and right there in front of the door he had hung himself. He was standing— not hanging—standing with his knees bent.[24]

Everyone was in a state of shock. The whole village was frightened. It hit Herman and Johann, Froese's sons, particularly hard. There had never been a suicide before in the village. It was the only time my father admitted in his stories to having been frightened. He went to his mother's room to sleep because his fears were keeping him awake. In Mennonite religious understanding, suicide was the ultimate sin, and according to tradition those who died by their own hands were not to be buried in the church cemetery. In the context of Stalinist Russia, such sensibilities no longer had currency. Although no letter is extant that directly reported these events, in a letter to Aganetha in the 1930s Anna noted, "I asked, and they consented to bury him in the church yard."[25]

Although my father's recounting of these events was always vivid, situating them in time was more difficult. My father placed the death of Froese a year or more after they had returned from Moscow when they were already part of the collective farm established at the time. The story he told was that Froese had a job tending the collective farm's horses. However, my conversations with his sister Katya placed Froese's suicide on 8 February 1930, just over a month after they returned from Moscow.

For my father, the suicide of his stepfather was always a turning point in his stories of growing up in Siberia. His stories often hinged on whether some event had been before or after the attempted escape to Moscow. After the death of his stepfather, he always placed himself in the role of the senior male member of an otherwise helpless family. That was likely not the case in the early 1930s, and his stories might have overemphasized his role to create that version of himself.

⟨⚬⟩

The memories of our childhood are often more prominent than the relatively brief period of time they represent. For Hans, the first twelve or thirteen years of his life were remembered as a time of personal challenges but not a time of great tragedy. Certainly the trip to Moscow was remembered as an adventure. The letters of his mother, who lost a daughter, and then a husband through tragic circumstances, portray much more poignantly the depth of the family's trauma. As a boy growing up amid the trauma, my father cast his stories as those of a survivor. These years would also have been the time for his mother to tell him about his father and the Werner family. Either the times interfered with such storytelling by his mother, or he forgot the stories. The suicide of his stepfather emerged most prominently in the stories of his growing-up years. Few stories, however, conveyed a sense of the rhythms of daily life in his family or village. Neil Sutherland suggests that childhood memories follow the lines of patterned scripts: school, neighbourhood, chores, and other domestic routines.[26] My father's scripts were seriously disrupted by the waves of instability brought on by the cholera epidemic and the suicide of his stepfather. Although childhood memories are often fragmented, likely the lack of stability contributed to even greater loss of narrative coherence in the stories of his childhood. Adolescence brought a greater awareness of the world around Hans, and his stories of the failed attempt to escape Stalin's Russia coincided with his entry into adolescence and a time when he would adapt to the Soviet system and to a large extent make it work for him.

3

Ivan, Stalin's Hope

BY 11 DECEMBER 1929, some 2,350 of those who had gone to Moscow, most of whom were Mennonite, had been returned to their villages on the Kulunda Steppe. Their determination to emigrate was not quelled, however, by this apparent failure. Throughout the winter and spring of 1930, local functionaries of the Stalinist regime tried to cope with continuing passive resistance by Mennonites who remained determined to emigrate rather than join the collective farms being established. Those who had returned to their villages from Moscow refused to accept seed grain, turned away offers of credit to put in crops, and sometimes did not reoccupy their own homes, choosing to stay in temporary quarters, all so that there would be nothing in the way of getting away quickly. The local government in Slavgorod even attempted to have their possessions returned to them for the same price they had sold them, an impossibility given that they had spent the proceeds on passports and that in most cases the purchasers could not be located.[1]

Opposition to forced collectivization was not peculiar to Mennonites but had become general by the spring of 1930. In the face of near revolution in the countryside, Stalin published his famous "Dizzy with Success" article in newspapers on 2 March 1930, in which he blamed regional functionaries for excesses in the drive for collectivization while claiming the 50 percent level that apparently had been achieved to be a great success.[2] Although the article signalled a temporary easing of the pace of forced collectivization, it was hardly noticeable to the Mennonite farmers of Siberia. The Slavgorod area, where Mennonites made up a large part of the German population, continued to experience dramatic declines in its agricultural economy. By June 1930, declines in the numbers of horses, cattle, sheep, and hogs ranged from 32 to 88 percent, higher than the already staggering losses in the region more generally.[3]

In spite of the apparent step backward from the use of force, Mennonite resistance to the state grew in intensity throughout the spring and early summer of 1930, coming to a head in late June. On 19 June, a meeting was held in Alexandrovka in the centre of the Mennonite settlement near Slavgorod to which the secretary of the regional party committee was invited. When he failed to appear, the meeting elected a chair and proceeded to collect names to make up a list of those wishing to emigrate. The list was confiscated by the late-arriving party officials, resulting in Mennonite women in the group trying to tear the briefcases with the documents out of their hands as they rode off. The next day a larger group made up mostly of Mennonite women gathered at the regional government offices in Halbstadt to demand return of the documents. Although their demand was not met, officials called for a meeting on 27 June of delegates from the entire German-speaking region that would include members of the collectives as well as independent farmers. In the Mennonite villages, rumours spread that regional party officials had been authorized to allow emigration, and on the morning of 27 June over 1,800 people showed up for the meeting. When officials tried to restrict participation in the meeting to appointed delegates only, the crowd entered the building, pulled tables outside, and demanded an open meeting. They elected a chair, Katharina Siemens, a health-care worker and daughter of a former Mennonite schoolteacher. The election of a woman as chair might have been seen as a way of forestalling the retribution that would follow if they elected male leaders. The meeting passed resolutions against anti-religious education and requested permission to emigrate. This display of public opposition demanded action by the party, and a number of the leaders of the mass demonstration were arrested. On 2 July, the arrest of one particular participant touched off another demonstration in front of government offices in Halbstadt. The crowd ultimately entered the back doors of the building, dragged out the arresting GPU (Soviet State Police) officer, and demanded that he call his supervisors to convey their demand that the individual be released. They subsequently also took a party official as hostage. The arrival of an armed twenty-person unit of the GPU finally ended the standoff, and, not surprisingly, numerous arrests followed, including that of Katharina Siemens.[4]

These dramatic events in the Halbstadt area were largely unnoticed in the Froese family. It is clear, however, that resistance to the new regime was also present among the Froeses, at least before Johann committed suicide. My grandmother's first letter to her daughter in Canada after the family was sent back from Moscow held out the possibility of another attempt "in a month or six weeks, possibly in spring, but hopefully in winter."[5] My father also recalled the events in Halbstadt somewhat because some participants who had fled the scene tried to avoid arrest by hiding in their village. However, for my father's family, the suicide of Johann and the pressing need to find some way to survive meant their attention was focussed on their own problems.

Having lost almost everything in the attempted escape via Moscow, and with the subsequent loss of husband and father, there was no other option for Anna and her children but to join the collective farm. Joining it was not automatic, however. My father recalled that they had to beg to be allowed to become members. The Moscow adventure and Johann Froese's strident anti-collectivization rhetoric had given them what Orlando Figes terms a "spoilt biography."[6] But they had nothing, and by joining the collective farm they could receive the basic food allocation that collectives had been instructed to extend to poor and mid-level peasants who joined them. It also meant a move away from their home in Grigorevka, still resisting collectivization, to neighbouring Markovka, already collectivized. For my grandmother, entry into the collective farm was obviously an embarrassment. When she described the harvest in a letter to her daughter and the Loewens, who had adopted her, she added, "of course, we didn't seed alone for ourselves, but rather two villages together."[7]

The return from Moscow also marked the gradual decline of my grandmother's prominence in my father's stories. Not surprisingly, since Hans was becoming an adolescent, he began to identify more with his peers than with his mother. The state also had a greater grip on his imagination through school and its activities. Although he continued to be called Hans at home, in his life away from home he became known as Ivan. Much of this had to do with his return to school. He remembered school as being easy, and because he was older he progressed through two levels in one year. But school had changed; instruction was now all in Russian, and it was likely in school that Hans became Ivan Ivanevich.

Of much greater interest to Ivan than academic subjects at school were programs designed to foster the technical skills demanded by the rapid industrialization of the Soviet Union. The early 1930s were the years of the first five-year plan that was to transform the Soviet Union into an industrial power able to defend the revolution against "capitalist encirclement," as Stalin put it.[8] In Ivan's school, a Russian teacher organized a glider club that built an actual flying glider, and Ivan was an active and enthusiastic participant. The project was probably the beginning of his lifelong interest in airplanes and flying. The club was regional in scope, and the boys who participated came from schools in the surrounding villages. During the winter, they took home pieces of wood to carve into specific shapes to make the parts of the glider. Ivan's hobby was whittling, and with his developing interest in mechanical things, the glider club was everything the adolescent boy could have wanted. The glider was completed during the winter, and the next summer the boys were actually able to fly it. The method of propelling the glider into the air was ingenious. Relying on a small hill and a large rubber band, the entire club pushed back the glider to stretch out the band, and when released, the glider achieved enough speed to become airborne. With the thermals created by the heat of the black fields providing the necessary lift, the glider gained altitude and could remain aloft almost indefinitely. The experience of flying was sheer joy for young Ivan.

His interest in airplanes might also have been stimulated by the arrival near their village of the first airplane anyone had ever seen. One day Ivan and the other boys heard the sound of an engine in the sky. Motorized vehicles were still a rarity, and no one had ever heard an engine in the sky. The boys ran out onto the nearby field where the airplane had landed, and the pilot asked them how to get to the neighbouring village. The boys were very excited, but their elders were sure the end of the world was at hand.

Ivan attended school for two years after the family returned from Moscow, and then at age fourteen, while still attending school during the day, he began working on the collective farm. Although the plan for collectivization included mechanizing agriculture, horses still provided the power for most farming activities. Ivan's first job was to drive four horses harnessed to a drive wheel that powered the threshing machines. His job was to stand on a small platform on the hub of a large wheel that had a horse harnessed to each spoke. Ivan stood on the turning platform with a whip to keep the horses moving, turning the wheel, and thus powering the threshing machine. He remembered helping the local miller take out panels in the windmill's vanes when the wind picked up. He also helped him sharpen the stones and did other odd jobs around the mill. It did not take long for him to be more formally employed on the collective farm, and he was soon the main breadwinner of the family. During the first two years in the collective, he plowed with three horses and a "slant" plow. The collective farm paid higher wages for skilled workers, and, according to his account, Ivan managed the equipment well, and the summers produced good earnings for the family.

By the end of 1931, the drive toward collectivization was substantially complete, and the Siberian countryside, including its Mennonite farmers, had largely given itself over to collective agriculture. Three forms of collectives were possible. The Association for the Cultivation of Land (TOZ) was essentially a fieldwork cooperative in which the farmers did their fieldwork together and divided the proceeds according to each farmer's contribution of land, equipment, and time. The second form was the *artel*, in which the farmers kept their home, garden, and some livestock but pooled all their other resources of land, labour, horses, and equipment. The third type was the commune, in which everything except personal effects was transferred to the collective. Mennonite farmers were most opposed to the commune system because it compromised their independence and threatened their ability to control the non-Mennonite influences on their children.

The return from Moscow and the suicide of Froese hastened the departure from home of the older Froese boys. Johann married shortly after the rest of the family returned, and Herman spent a lot of time away from home. My father believed him to be a genius when it came to numbers and playing cards, and in addition to his work in the collective Herman spent a lot of time travelling to various clubs where he played cards for money. Although not condoned in traditional Mennonite practice, the family sometimes benefited from his gambling activities. Although not explicit about what Herman did, in a letter likely written in 1932, Anna reported to her daughter in Canada that Herman "was at our place for a while, not even the entire winter. Today he bought ten *pud* of potatoes for two rubles per *pud*, but we still don't have nearly enough potatoes."[9] In the same letter, Anna reported that a wave of typhus had swept through the village. In her letter to Aganetha, she reported that Ivan had been sick with typhus for fifteen days but was up and around again, though still weak and thin.[10] My father recalled he was so weak he had to stop for a rest when he took the short walk to visit the neighbours.

Anna's concern about having enough food signalled the beginnings of what would become a full-fledged famine in the winter of 1932–33. Along with Stalin's forced collectivization drive, there were relentless demands for grain from the newly created collectives. The famine was not caused by drought, crop failure, or problems of distribution; rather, as Robert Tucker puts it, "the man at the centre" was Stalin himself.[11] My father remembered the unrelenting drive for more grain; the authorities "always wanted more from the kolkhoz, always more. Always more, and there was nothing."[12] The family's food supplies dwindled until there was nothing left. In January 1933, Ivan turned sixteen, and he and his friends were old enough to fend for themselves in the deteriorating food supply conditions. Early each morning during that spring, Ivan and his friends Henry Matthies, Abram Martens, and Jakob Wiebe left home to spend all day searching for food. Whatever they found they shared. One story my father often repeated was how they went into the wetlands to search for duck eggs. He was sure their parents would have been afraid for their lives had they known the lengths to which the boys went to get food. The area was so soggy that they could not walk on the swamp, so they took their clothes off on solid ground, and by rolling into the swamp they distributed their weight over a wide enough area to stay above the water. If they were lucky enough to catch a duck, it was immediately eviscerated, wrapped in clay, and baked in a fire. Finding duck eggs was more likely, and Ivan and the rest of the family survived off the eggs and other food he found and brought home. They also picked sorrel, which his mother used to make a thin soup. The sweepings from granaries and the cracked grain and weed seeds set aside for pigeons also became food—at least if they could be kept away from the grain collectors.

For Ivan and the rest of the family, the famine ended when the whole village turned out with pitchforks to spear the fish that came up the creeks to spawn. Some of them were trapped in the pools left behind by the receding water and were easily harvested. They were carried home in baskets and smoked in the chimney to become the main staple until the regime finally relented on grain procurements and the new crop was harvested. Ivan's memories of smelling and tasting rye bread when it became available again were particularly vivid. His stories of the famine were centred entirely on himself. Other than his references to bringing home eggs and picking sorrel, my father never mentioned how the rest of the family, or other villagers, fared during the spring and early summer of 1933. He did say that no one in the village died as a result of the famine.

The *artel* form of collective, the most common in Mennonite areas, evolved in the 1930s to a system that compensated its peasant members on the basis of piecework. Each type of work on the collective farm, such as plowing, combining, or harrowing, was assigned a certain number of *trudanye* or "labour days." For instance, someone in charge of running a combine, one of the most valued skills in rural areas, might earn three or four labour days for each actual day of work, depending on how much grain was harvested that day. At the end of the season, the collective's members were paid according to the number of trudanye they had accumulated. They received a share of what was left after the collective had delivered its allocation to the state, kept back seed for the next year, and paid its bills. Members were usually paid in kind—a certain number of kilograms of wheat per trudanye; or quantities of sunflower oil, in the case of crops not consumed directly. Occasionally, in good years, a cash payment might be paid out in proportion to the number of trudanye a member had accumulated. The amounts received could vary greatly depending on the effectiveness of the collective farm's management, the vagaries of the weather, and the state's grain procurement policies. For example, in the concentrated German settlement area north of Slavgorod, collective farmers received between 2.1 and 15.0 kilograms of grain per trudanye in 1934.[13] The aim of collectivization was to replace small and fragmented horse-powered agriculture with large mechanized farms. To achieve this transformation, the regime created the machine tractor station (MTS). It was a second-tier collective that performed all of the mechanized tasks that required tractors for a number of collective farms. The MTS charged the collectives for its services in kind—wheat, vegetable oil, and other produce.

After finishing school, Ivan became an active participant in the MTS. In the winter of 1933–34, he went to the nearby town of Kulunda to receive both training and experience in operating and repairing agricultural equipment. In the spring of 1934, Ivan no longer worked for an individual collective farm but for the MTS. Each winter he returned to Kulunda for further training and repair work. As a *tractorist*, he could earn three trudanye for each day worked plus a cash bonus at the end of the year. When he became a *combinyor*, or combine operator, his earnings rose even more. The combine operator was in charge of a tractor that pulled two combines. The process was still not entirely mechanized because each combine had a person, usually a young woman, who sat on a seat above the header and raised and lowered it manually. My father told stories about how he worried that the girls would fall into the cutting knife when the days got long and they became sleepy. Combinyors got paid according to the number of hectares and the amount of grain they harvested. It meant one had to go as fast as possible but not so fast that the combine became overloaded, resulting in poor separation and too much grain ending up with the chaff on the ground behind the machine. According to my father, the combinyor was the highest-paid position in rural Russia, matching and often exceeding the pay of the *brigadier*, or manager, of the collective farm. The rise in earnings finally put the family on a reasonable economic footing. But it meant working hard. In one letter to her daughter Aganetha, Anna excused Ivan for not writing to her because "your brother is at work every day, only on Sunday he is at home."[14]

By the mid-1930s, there were signs that the Soviet Union might finally step back from a constant state of revolution. In 1935, Stalin pronounced that "life has become better, comrades. Life has become more joyous…and when life is joyous, work goes well."[15] Although the drive to make the Soviet Union a military force through industrialization would continue, in the mid-1930s life was less austere than during the early days of the revolution. Along with more consumer goods and perks for meritorious workers, there was more fun. Dancing, condemned in earlier times, was now encouraged. Ivan and his friends were models for the new outlook. The young people of the village led a busy social life in which Ivan and his friends were active participants. He came by his musical talent honestly, but now he played the balalaika at dances rather than the hymns his grandfather had played on the violin on warm summer evenings. Since his stories of those days were often told in the context of the Mennonite community of Steinbach, the stories of playing for dances were somewhat muted, and one always sensed there was more to be told. Dancing was not considered an appropriate activity for the Mennonites of Steinbach in the 1960s and 1970s.

The possibilities for increased social interaction made possible a memorable trip for Ivan and his family. In the fall of 1935, the family, and others from the village, made a trip to the Eighties Villages to visit family and friends. The trip was important in my father's memories and was mentioned in his mother's letters to her daughter Aganetha in Canada. In a letter in which Anna described the trip, she seemed somewhat embarrassed to admit that they were no longer independent farmers. She noted that they "drove to Silberfeld with a truck. We bought a vehicle last year, a group of us."[16] Ivan

Ivan and two friends, Jakob Wiebe and Abram Friesen, posing with their instruments in 1934. Although his stories most often referred to playing the balalaika, here he is the one in the middle of the photo holding a guitar.

was the driver of the truck, though it belonged not to their collective farm but to the MTS. While in Silberfeld, Anna visited her sister, who had returned from an attempt to flee collectivization by going to the Amur River region. My father vividly remembered visiting at the home of his aunt, Tina (Werner) Hinz, which provided the context for a story of having danced with his cousin, who had kept the fact that they were cousins secret from her boyfriend. As he recalled,

> The girls were very nice, they took me along to their friends; one of them said—she had a boyfriend—that she would really confuse him. She took my arm, and we went to the dance. These were German colonists; they were all Lutherans. We came there, and she sat with me and put her arm around me, and her boyfriend came. She said, "Look, there he comes." I told her that I hoped I wouldn't get into a fight with him; he had such a long face! He came to us and said, "What's this?" She laughed and then introduced us, indicating that we were cousins. We sat down, and he was a fine person; it was a bit of a joke.[17]

Aganetha (Neufeld) Werner, Ivan's grandmother, standing beside her sister.

The "cousin" of his memory was likely Maria, a year younger than Ivan and the stepdaughter of his aunt and no relation to him. According to Anna's letter, Ivan's grandmother, Aganetha (Neufeld) Werner, had also been visiting in the Eighties Villages but had already returned to Nikolaipol. Ivan took the truck and continued on to Nikolaipol to visit her. It was the only time he ever saw his grandmother.

> I was there possibly an hour, because I went there alone...with the truck. It was in the garden, she was hoeing, she was in her eighties, she was hoeing, she came along the path, she didn't know who I was. I had been four years old when we moved away from there. She looked at me.... I said, "Don't you know me?" "No," she said. I said, "I am Hans Werner." She said, "That little four-year-old boy?" "Yes," I said, "that's who I am." Well, we went inside and had a cup of coffee, and she told me that I was the only Werner left that she knew about, and I was supposed to see to it that the family name didn't become extinct. She told me various things about my father, and she mentioned some things about my grandfather—and I had to leave again. From there, I went back to the Eighties Villages.[18]

There were also possibilities for rewards for good performance at work. Although my father was never entirely clear about what exactly he had done, sometime in either 1936 or 1937 he was honoured for his performance in exceeding the norms for a *tractorist* and *combinyor*. He recalled with great pride his methods of fine-tuning equipment so that it worked at maximum efficiency. He had devised a system of tuning the tractor's fuel–air mixture until just the right amount of blue flame appeared above the exhaust pipe at night. It meant the tractor was producing maximum power using the least amount of fuel. His diligence likely won him the award—a trip to Moscow and coupons to purchase consumer goods, likely at the Torgsin stores, which required hard currency. Ivan made the trip to Moscow alone and came back with a variety of consumer goods. He never explained how the community reacted to the honour bestowed on him, but it seemed he had purchased a large amount of cloth that was distributed throughout the village and helped to relieve the chronic lack of clothing that plagued the Siberian villages.

On the night of 30 August 1935, a Donbass coal miner named Alexei Stakhanov mined 102 tonnes of coal, a record that exceeded by almost fifteen times the norm of 7.3 tonnes for a six-hour shift. The event marked the beginning of the Stakhanovite movement, in which Stalin created a series of merit awards to honour overachievement in work performance. The Stakhanovite movement also signalled a new attempt by Stalin to woo non-party members. In a 1935 speech, he suggested "one can be a Bolshevik without being a Party member."[19] Some years after my taped interviews with my father, I was reading about the Stakhanovite movement and casually asked him if he had ever heard of it. He replied that he had and went on to say that the reward of a trip to Moscow came with the honour of being a Stakhanovite.

While winters in Ivan's early years at the MTS were spent in training, in later years Ivan would drive a truck transporting various agricultural products and supplies. My father enjoyed telling the story of one of these trips when he travelled into the forests some distance south of the Pashnaya villages to pick up a load of lumber for the kolkhoz. He recalled driving through many Russian villages with their large numbers of dogs not accustomed to the noise and dust of trucks passing through. Inevitably a few dogs got run over in each village, and to avoid the wrath of villagers they continued without stopping. They spent the night deep in the forest at the home of a forest ranger. In the evening, the ranger's wife bustled about providing a meal for them and preparing a place for them to sleep. In the morning when they awoke, she was already in the kitchen preparing breakfast for them. The story's surprise ending related how the ranger announced at the breakfast table that during the night they had been blessed with an addition to the family. It had not been apparent to Ivan and his companions that the woman who had served them had been in the last stages of pregnancy.

In the late 1930s, Stalin unleashed what historians have called the "Great Purge." During the purge, millions of people were arrested, many of them were executed, and others were sent to the gulag. My father told very few stories of arrests in the village of Markovka, though sprinkled throughout his casual references to individuals were comments about them having been arrested. The miller, a Mr. Wiebe, whom he had helped as a fourteen-year-old boy, was arrested for sabotage when the mill burned down in the later 1930s. He had left the mill with the wind vane's panels in place and the gears engaged. During the night, the wind had picked up, and the friction brake had set the mill on fire. Almost incidental was a brief reference to the arrest of thirty men and one woman in their village on an afternoon in 1936 or 1937. The arrests emanated from the discovery of an alleged plot in which the *brigadiers* of the collective and the MTS had collaborated to seed 100 hectares of land outside the plan. That meant the harvest from the land could bypass the state's procurement system and be distributed directly to the collective's members based on trudanye. The increasing threat of arrest in the later 1930s was likely also responsible for the end of letters to Canada. The last letter Ivan's sister Aganetha received from her mother was dated September 1935—after that, all contact between Aganetha and her mother was lost.

The threat of arrest was likely also the source of my father's memory of being sent to bury a "Werner" book. Ivan was instructed by his mother to bury a thick book, "like a Bible," bound with a wooden frame, that she indicated would incriminate all the Werners and provide evidence for their arrest. As later evidence would reveal, my father created a story to fill in gaps in the history of his ancestors based on this memory. Although he acknowledged he never thought to look into the book, he believed it contained evidence that the Werners had been wealthy landlords in south Russia. "The Werners had been rich at one time in Ukraine. My great-grandfather had owned a lot of land. Wernersdorf—Werner's *khutor*—belonged to this land. Afterwards it was land that was rented out, everybody rented it and paid him rent, in the first years. Later on it was sold and divided into villages. How it turned out later—I have no idea."[20] There might have been a hope to recover the book someday, because Ivan wrapped it in wax paper and then put it into a burlap bag and buried it in a deep hole behind their barn.

When I asked my father whether his mother had been a happy person, he acknowledged that after the jolts of losing her daughter, the failed trip to Moscow, the death of her husband, and forced collectivization, she had rarely smiled or laughed. In spite of her unhappiness, "sometimes [you] could notice that she had been happy at one time." In one particular memory, Ivan came home to the sound of her playing the small accordion she had received as a wedding gift. With one foot on a chair, she was playing a brisk polka on the instrument usually reserved for playing hymns. It was one of the few times in the 1930s that my father could remember her laughing and enjoying herself.[21]

By the later 1930s, Ivan was a young man—his twentieth birthday was in 1937. With the older Froese children marrying and starting their own families, he assumed the role of both breadwinner and authority in the Froese household. But the fabric of family life and moral codes that had governed Mennonite life had been considerably frayed by the events of the previous fifteen years. My father recalled having to go to his sister Katya's room at two in the morning one night to suggest it was time for her suitor to leave. Katya was thirteen, and her suitor was Abram Isaac, a boy a few years older to whom she would be briefly married.

I never took particular note at the time, but my father's stories of these years never mentioned any interest in girls. Even though my father portrayed himself as being active in the social circles of his village, playing at dances, visiting the neighbours, and attending community events, he never mentioned any girlfriends. The reason for the absence of such stories only became clear many years later. In the summer of 1990, I travelled to Germany with my parents to visit my father's sisters, Katya and Martha, who had come to Germany as part of the large migration of Soviet Germans after the fall of the Berlin Wall and the subsequent collapse of the Soviet Union. On a Sunday morning, we were at the Darmstadt Baptist Church, where both my father's sisters attended and where my aunt Katya would meet her first husband, Abram Isaac, again. The marriage to Isaac had failed soon after it was solemnized, and a lot had transpired before the awkward "reunion" in the church lobby in 1990. After a brief conversation between them, Isaac came to talk to me since we were both standing somewhat apart from the group, which included my parents, my father's sister Katya and her husband Johann, and his other sister Martha. Isaac casually commented that it really was too bad about my father's first wife but added that there really was nothing else my father could have done.

Although he told so many stories of his life, he never, not before or after, intimated that he had been married before he met and married my mother. In my search for documentation on aspects of his later German military record, I had come across evidence suggesting he had been married in occupied Poland, but the casual remark in the lobby of the Darmstadt church was a surprise. If Orlando Figes's suggestion that the "intermingling of myth and memory sustains every family" is true, then it must also include the myths created by memories never revealed in the stories told.[22] My father seemingly could never find a narrative that included the story of his previous marriages without destroying the "myth" he was creating about himself. In 1990, I was not sure even my mother knew. By then, she had also told me the story of her first husband, who had disappeared during the war. In the 1950s, a few years after marrying my father, she had found out from a mutual relative that her first husband had survived the war, had remarried, and was living in what was then East Germany.

I never asked my father about the first marriage, but during other visits with my relatives in Germany and with my mother after his death some details emerged. Ivan married Anna Loewen, likely in 1938. My aunt Katya considered her an attractive woman, with "a beautiful face," and Ivan had dated her for some time. The marriage ceremony reflected more difficult times than those of the mid-1930s. Katya recalled that she had canvassed the village for an appropriate shirt to borrow since Ivan had no dress shirt to wear to the ceremony. The wedding was a double ceremony with his friend Jakob Wiebe and fiancée Susanna, and it was a civic affair held in the *selsoviet* in the nearby village of Annanyevka. In hindsight, it was likely fortuitous, but possibly also surprising, that no pregnancy seems to have resulted from the three months the couple was married before Ivan was drafted into the Red Army.

The ambitious five-year plans, collectivization, and the emphasis on modernizing Soviet society had been in part to prepare the Soviet Union militarily. People such as Ivan had been Stalin's hope for the day when the Soviet Union would be a strong industrial and military force. The fateful notice to appear before the Soviet equivalent of a draft board likely came in the summer of 1938, a month or so after Ivan had married Anna. The notice required that he and three others from the village appear before the board in Klyuchi, the seat of local government. The three young men travelled together in a horse-drawn vehicle supplied by the kolkhoz. My father recalled being asked a seemingly simple question, whether or not he was willing to serve the motherland. Certainly by this time any notion of being a pacifist, or requesting military exemption on religious grounds, was not part of his awareness and would not, in any case, be comprehended under Stalinism. Ivan knew there could be only one answer, that he would be honoured to serve if deemed worthy. The process of being drafted included an examination by six or seven doctors and some questions to which the answers were already known, since it seemed a lot of documentation about him had already been collected. Two other young men from the village, his friend Abram Martens and a fellow he only remembered as having the last name Kroeker, were drafted at the same time. At the end of the process, they were pronounced to be healthy, told they had been drafted into the Red Army, and advised that a notice of when and where to appear would be sent to them in a couple of weeks.

Ivan went home to continue the harvest, and a few weeks later the notice arrived that he was to appear at the train station at Kulunda on a certain day in October 1938. He worked at the harvest until the evening before he left, and early the next day he was on his way to be at the station by eight. There he met other draftees from neighbouring villages, and they all boarded the train for points and futures they could not have imagined. My father recalled that he had not been particularly concerned about the draft because the term of service was three years, and they all expected to return home after that. One of the few times he showed some emotion during our conversations was when he admitted that, once the train was under way and the initial excitement was over, "it struck you that you might never come back."[23]

The train made its way westward toward the Urals, picking up new recruits at many of the stations along the Trans-Siberian Railway. My father remembered it being a quiet trip—not much was said; some of the Russian recruits sang; Ivan, Martens, and Kroeker talked quietly. The train's ultimate destination was a military base near the city of Kirov in European Russia. By the time the train reached Kirov, some 400 new recruits had been picked up. Once there, boot camp began. Ivan and the others were lined up in rows of four and marched into the barracks. That first day they were still civilians, but it would be the last day for some time.

⊸⊸⊸○ ◯⊸⊸

My father constructed his narratives of this period in his life in ways suggesting that it was in large part due to his efforts that the surviving remnant of the Werner family recovered from the disaster of the failed emigration of 1929 and the subsequent suicide of Johann Froese. Comparisons with my grandmother's letters and later revelations point to how his stories became much more selective. Most apparent was the complete absence of references to his first marriage. The separation from his wife that resulted from the war must have been more than just a painful loss. My father must have felt considerable guilt about his role in that separation.

His stories were also told in the context of Cold War Canada, where the Soviet Union was the embodiment of everything evil. It meant that my father had to balance his own story's plot of successful participation in Soviet society with the reality of the evil represented by that society in the social context of his listeners. More careful examination of his stories suggests that, to a large extent, my father was not only Ivan in the world beyond his family. He had also come to terms personally with the Soviet system and had found ways to make it work for him. Although he was not a political person, he must have quietly shaken his head at the "old ways" of people such as his stepfather and uncles. Ivan could see that the new regime would survive and that continued resistance would only lead to further suffering and ruin. By the end of the 1930s, the faith of his Mennonite forebears seems to have been far from his mind. Ivan had become part of the Soviet system even though he did not believe in its ideology, and he had left behind the faith and sensibilities of his Mennonite past.

The Mist Clears

Until the 1990s, it seemed that the inaccessibility of the Soviet Union and its records and the seeming impossibility of connecting with family that remained there meant that any further Werner history would never be recovered. My father had found ways to construct a narrative of the Werner family that was coherent with the fragments of memory of what he had been told. The collapse of communism in the early 1990s and the emigration of ethnic Germans in its wake raised new possibilities for competing narratives to emerge. In 1997, some sixty years after my father had left his family and Siberia behind, he received a call from a Heinrich Froese, a son of my father's stepbrother who was travelling in Canada and wanted to pay him a visit. My father did not know Froese, who was part of the large migration of Soviet Germans that flooded into Germany and was now looking for his roots. Heinrich had never known his own father, who had died when Heinrich was young. In the course of the conversation with him, my father related the story about the visit to his grandmother and the Hinz family. Froese responded that he knew a Hinz family that had emigrated from the Soviet Union and promised to connect with them when he got back to Germany. The encounter with Froese and the reference to a Hinz relative proved to be fortuitous. Not only were the Hinzes in Germany relatives, but the Tina (Werner) Hinz my father had visited in the 1930s had written a memoir that had been preserved by her descendants. It tells a story my father could not tell.

The memoir tells the story of my father's ancestors. The memoirist's
father and my great-grandfather was Johann Werner, born in a suburb near
the Black Sea port city of Berdyansk in 1856. My great-grandmother was
Aganetha Neufeld from the village of Steinfeld in the large Molotschna
Mennonite settlement. Later references in the memoir suggest that this
might have been Aganetha's second marriage. Tina mentions half-brothers
named Warkentin, but they must have lived elsewhere since there is no mention of them living with the Werner family. The courtship of Johann and
Aganetha is a recollected story of what Tina remembered being told by her
parents. Aganetha had come to visit her brother in Berdyansk, where she met
Johann. Johann, his father Johann, and his uncles Heinrich and Jakob were
all factory workers. After their marriage, both Johann and Aganetha worked
for a few years in Berdyansk before they moved to the village of her parents,
where Johann worked in a windmill. He then made parts for wagons and
seed-cleaning mills for the Jacob Rennpenning factories of Fabrikerwiese in
the Mennonite Molotschna colony.[1] Johann made the wooden parts at home
and delivered them to the factory, where the metal parts were added before assembly. Tina was born in 1898, when her father was in his mid-forties. By that
year, the family was about to join the growing numbers of Mennonite workers
who had no land and no prospect of becoming farmers. Johann changed his
work again when he was hired to work on a nearby estate as manager. The
job paid well, but Johann was out of work again when the estate was sold. It
meant another change of workplace and a move to a nearby village, where he
did finishing carpentry for a Catholic priest in charge of a church being built
there. To supplement the resources needed for a growing family, the children
helped with opening silkworm cocoons to make silk in the winter. A wealthy
Jewish family who lived in the village also provided some paid work for Tina
and her brother. On the Sabbath, the two of them went to light the lamps in
their large home; they were paid three rubles a month for their work.

Johann Werner's father and brothers had moved to Siberia sometime before 1906, and in December of that year Johann also decided to move and join
them to finally realize the dream of being his own master. His wife Aganetha
was opposed to the move, and as Tina recalls he tried to persuade her by
asking if "the children should always only be servants for other people." That
prospect he said he could not bear and lamented that the two of them "live in
a stranger's house, have no garden, no land and have to be workers." Even if
the land in Siberia "was only rented land," it was better than what they had.[2]

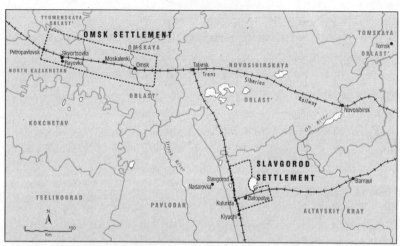

Map 2. Mennonite settlements in West Siberia.

The Werner family's move to Siberia was part of a large migration that established one of the largest daughter colonies of Mennonites in Russia. The Trans-Siberian Railway opened up vast areas of the West Siberian plain, and, not unlike the story of western Canadian settlement, the tsar needed settlers to make the railway viable. The first Mennonites moved to Siberia as individual families and established small villages or purchased large estates between Omsk and Petropavlovsk, along the railway line. It seems the senior Werner and Johann's brothers had settled on rented land near Petropavlovsk. Tina recalls that her family left Ukraine to join them in December, travelling in red railway cars that were often cold because they had only small stoves and were not insulated. Her father had sent his brothers some money, and they had rented a house for the family about seventy *verst* from the city of Petropavlovsk in the predominantly Mennonite village of Skvortsovka, where brother Jakob lived. The family had enough money left over to buy three horses and a cow to begin their new farming life. Johann's parents and brother Heinrich probably lived in a village approximately twenty-five verst away. Grandfather Werner is described as being big and tall, while Tina remembers her grandmother being a wisp of a woman.[3]

Johann had sold all of the family's furniture before the move, and his first task upon their arrival was to use his carpentry skills to refurnish the household. He also built basic farm equipment and in the spring began farming the land he had rented. The village was surrounded by forest, and Tina indicates her mother soon adjusted to the new environment, particularly because of the prolific wild berries that kept her busy canning jam all summer long. She reports that, even after that first summer of farming on their own, they had grain to sell; "we had bread, and my brothers and sisters did not have to be servants for strangers."[4]

In July 1908, during the second Siberian summer for the Werner clan, the younger Johann Werner, my grandfather, married Anna Janzen. The Janzens were a Mennonite family who had also moved to Siberia from Ukraine. After their marriage, the junior Johann and Anna continued to live with his parents until the fall, when free land became available on the Kulunda Steppe in the Barnaul area, some 700 kilometres southeast of where they had initially settled. Attracted by the possibility of actually owning their land, the senior Johann decided to make the long move to the Kulunda Steppe. The settlement the family decided to join would become one of the largest Mennonite settlements in Russia. Approximately 50,000 *desyatin*[5] of land were granted to Mennonites for settlement on the basis of each household receiving fifteen desyatin per adult male member. In addition, each settler family was promised fifty rubles when they moved onto their land and another fifty rubles when they improved the land by breaking up some of the native sod and constructing buildings.[6] After a trip to the area in the fall of 1908, Johann returned to report that he had drawn lots and received a parcel of land in a new village that would be called Nikolaipol. Mennonites had managed to negotiate an exception to the tsarist government's general rule that the land was to be distributed only on the basis of the number of adult males. Instead, Mennonites petitioned for and were granted permission to divide the amount of land they would be eligible for on the adult male basis equally among households. The resulting farm size ranged from fifty to sixty desyatin.

Johann Werner spent the winter trying to find a way to move all of their goods by rail, but since the new Mennonite settlement was not connected to the Trans-Siberian Railway he finally decided to make the journey by sleigh. During the winter, Johann and his boys built the sleighs, including one with a caboose-like enclosure to provide shelter for the family on the long trip. At this time, the family included Johann and his wife Aganetha, their son Johann and his wife Anna, and unmarried children Abram, Maria, Tina, and Jakob, the youngest. The senior Johann and the other Werner brothers remained behind in the Petropavlovsk area. In March, the caravan of three sleighs left Skvortsovko and travelled along the tracks to the city of Omsk. The family stayed in various homes along the way, as was the custom for travellers throughout nineteenth-century Russia. From Omsk, they turned south to follow the Irtysh River to the Pavlodar area. There, Tina reports, they stayed in the Mennonite village of Nadarovka for a day, and then travelled to the new town of Slavgorod, which at the time must have been little more than a few shacks.[7] They arrived at four in the afternoon on a Sunday in their new home village of Nikolaipol.

Even though Tina is retelling some of what can only have been told to her by others, her memory is vivid. At the time of the move to Nikolaipol, she was ten years old. She remembers, for instance, that the sleigh trip to Slavgorod took eighteen days. The first task when they got to the Nikolaipol village site was to build a sod hut; a proper house would follow. The sod had to be broken since the Kulunda Steppe had been home only to the Kirghiz and their herds. The Kirghiz were Turkic-speaking nomads who had been displaced by the tsar to allow for settlement by Europeans.

Nothing was seeded that first summer because the land was still native sod, and the family had to buy everything for the upcoming winter. In the fall, Jakob, the youngest son, died; of fourteen children born to Johann and Aganetha to that point, only five had survived. Fall also brought the second marriage in the family when daughter Maria married Franz Eckert from the village. My grandparents, Johann and Anna Werner, spent the winter with Anna's parents in a village near Slavgorod. Anna's brother and two sisters had contracted diphtheria, and all three died within a week. The oldest, Kornelius, was twenty-four, his sister Justina was twenty, and the youngest, Lena, was sixteen. The newly married couple spent the winter helping the aging parents. In spring, the senior Janzens moved to their other married children's home in the village of Silberfeld, and Johann and Anna returned to Nikolaipol. The summer of 1910 was busy for them. Their first child, also named Anna, was born, the newly broken land had to be seeded, and they built a barn and the typical Mennonite storage building, the *sheen*. The family all worked hard to make the clay bricks used to build these buildings.

During the next ten years, the Werner clan prospered. Tina remembers her parents having "luck with the livestock," which allowed them to advance economically. By 1913, she reports, they had "four cows, eight horses; God had blessed them."[8] By 1917, the younger Johann also had three horses, the four cows had become six, and with Johann's two cows and all the young stock the farm had become one of the more prosperous in the village. During the

First World War, the railway was extended from Tatarsk on the Trans-Siberian line to Slavgorod, making it much more profitable to grow grain to sell on the market for cash.

These were also the years when Tina became a young woman and was courted by one neighbour boy but fell in love with another. She was only fifteen when Isaac Regehr, son of a newly arrived family who lived across the street and her brother's friend, lingered after a visit to ask whether she would marry him. She turned him down because she thought she was too young. A few months later another neighbour boy, Jacob Reimer, came to tell her that he had been in love with her since childhood and wanted to marry her but was prepared to wait until she was older. After a few days of thinking about it, she consented. Her brother Abram married Maria Derksen from a nearby village, a marriage Tina opposed because he had promised a girl in Omsk that he would marry her. My grandfather Johann and grandmother Anna moved out of the family home to establish themselves in their own house nearby.

It was a time of vibrant church life. Tina reports glowingly on choir programs in which the women wore dresses they all had sewn from the same material and the men all wore black suits. She tells of how she was moved to commit herself to faith at an evening service conducted by a visiting minister. She attended classes at which they memorized the catechism, and she faced the question of whether to be baptized by pouring water on her head, as was done by the larger Kirchengemeinde, or by complete immersion in the river, as was the custom of the Mennonite Brethren. She must have chosen to remain with the Kirchengemeinde since its bishop, Jacob Gerbrandt, baptized her at a ceremony in the church in the village of Reinfeld. Although the names of ministers and the faith practices she describes are clearly Mennonite, the word *Mennonite* never appears in her memoir. Many former Mennonites in the Soviet Union became Baptists after 1955 and have no memory of a specifically Mennonite faith practice.[9]

There was also time for music and laughter. Everyone in the Johann Werner family was a musician. Tina mentions that she was the main voice in her section of the choir and that she played the guitar, zither, and harmonica. She remembers her father playing almost any instrument, while her mother was an accomplished singer. On an evening when the Werner house was full of visitors, Tina took the zither, and her friend from across the street the guitar, and they began singing. My grandparents joined them for a time before returning to help entertain the guests. Tina recalls that her parents loved singing and music, and the family sang every evening. It was a time of "joy and happiness." At dusk, when the workday had ended, her father took the violin, and the family sang and played. When it got dark, the lamps were lit, and everyone took out their handiwork.

Most people, she remembers, led upright lives and attended worship services. In contrast, in the memoir's accounts of the events of the First World War, the civil war that followed, and then collectivization, people's status as believers and unbelievers became more clearly stated, and in her estimation many lost their faith entirely. Her positive portrayal of the relationship with her father and brothers in the more carefree years before the First World War is characteristic of her portrayal of men generally. However, after the trauma and turmoil Tina experienced in the early 1920s, men in her memoir become more distant and less reliable. The male figures who represented security and safety before these events are portrayed thereafter as unfaithful; they are taken away from family and loved ones because of arrest and exile, or they die. Men generally can no longer be relied on.

Even before the First World War broke out, the Werner family's labour resources started to be taxed. Abram was drafted into the medical corps in the fall of 1913. He was stationed at Moskalenki along the Trans-Siberian Railway near Omsk and wrote to say that things were going well. News of the outbreak of the war in August 1914 shocked the entire village of Nikolaipol, and almost immediately all the adult males were called up for service. For Mennonites, service meant the medical corps or the forestry service that had been established as an alternative to military service for pacifist Mennonites. My grandfather Johann begged his father to assume responsibility for his family. He had also been called into service and would be stationed in Tomsk, where many Mennonite young men served as forestry workers.[10] By then, his family included three children: Anna, born in 1910, Sara in 1911, and Aganetha in 1914. The senior Johann was now in his late fifties, old enough for Tina to refer to him as elderly and not able to work as hard as he had before. The outbreak of the war and the loss of his sons to medical and forestry service meant the harvest would have to be gathered by the senior Johann and his wife, daughters, and daughters-in-law. Tina and her father attempted to cut the grain, but she could not handle the horses. With her father managing the horses, and with Tina and Anna, my grandmother, working at it together, they could manage the sheaves. After the grain was cut, Anna and Tina went to the fields to gather the sheaves, while her parents threshed the grain with a threshing stone in the yard. It was time consuming and difficult but possible. In the middle of it all, they got word that the senior Werner grandfather in Skvortsovko was dying.

Johann left the remainder of the harvest to the women. His wife took him to Slavgorod, where he took the train back to the village near Petropavlovsk, where the family's Siberian odyssey began. He arrived in time to see his father still alive, to visit with him briefly before he died, and to stay long enough to attend the funeral before returning to Nikolaipol. His father had lived to the ripe old age of ninety-two and had been active until a week before his death.

Because of his father's age and the fact that there were no other males around, the younger Johann, my grandfather, obtained leave from alternative service to return home most years to help with the harvest and during seeding. On Christmas day 1917, Johann and Anna had another child, my father, whom they named Hans. Johann might have already returned home permanently from his forestry service to be present at the birth because by then the Bolsheviks were in control and had withdrawn Russia from the war. In March 1918, Tina married Jakob Reimer, the neighbour boy from across the street with whom she had fallen in love five years earlier. The Werner clan continued to grow, and by 1919 my grandfather Johann had built his own home in the village, and his brother Abram had moved into the house on the senior Werner's yard. The senior Johann also began reducing his own farming activities by giving land to his two sons. In 1920, he seeded only three *desyatin*, but the village farmers threshed his grain to grind into flour because their own was not yet ripe. Their own supply from the previous year had all been taken by the ruthless grain requisitions of the new Bolshevik regime.

The turmoil that engulfed Russia during the First World War hardly appears at all in Tina Hinz's memoir. The war went increasingly badly for Russia, and in February 1917 riots broke out in the capital of Petrograd, as St. Petersburg had been renamed at the beginning of the war. The riots led to the February Revolution in which the tsar abdicated and a provisional government took over with the intention of establishing a liberal democracy. The provisional government kept Russia in an unpopular war, and in the workers' councils, or soviets, Lenin's Bolshevik Party gained the upper hand. The October 1917 Bolshevik Revolution brought to power the Communist Party, as the Bolsheviks had renamed themselves. Lenin's party signed the Treaty of Brest-Litovsk and took Russia out of the war. For the next three years, however, Russia would be embroiled in civil war.

In Siberia, the new regime quickly gained a modicum of power, and by February 1918 the towns and cities along the Trans-Siberian Railway were in Bolshevik hands. Bolshevik control, however, would be short lived. By June 1918, anti-Bolshevik forces assisted by Czech prisoners of war controlled Siberia. In a coup later that year, a formal White regime came to power under Admiral Kolchak, who installed himself as dictator. For a time, Siberia was an independent region. That situation ended when the Red Army crossed the Ural Mountains in 1919. The clash between the Bolshevik Red Army and Kolchak's White Army was as intense in Siberia as the contest between the Whites and Reds elsewhere in Russia. On 15 January 1920, Kolchak was captured at Irkutsk and eventually executed. West Siberia was once again firmly under Bolshevik control.[11]

The events of the civil war took place primarily in the cities along the Trans-Siberian Railway. The Mennonite villages near Slavgorod were not entirely spared, however. In September 1918, disenchanted German peasants in Podsosnovo, a Lutheran German village not far from Nikolaipol, aligned themselves with Ukrainian peasants who had settled in nearby Cherno Dol to organize a revolt against the brutal White regime. The uprising was stimulated by an order mobilizing those born in 1898 and 1899 for service in the White Army. One thousand peasants gathered in Cherno Dol on 1 September, and in the early morning hours they left for Slavgorod, where they encircled the city and drove out the White Army detachment stationed there. They released political prisoners held in the city and then went home, leaving local Bolshevik sympathizers to set up a revolutionary government. Reaction from Omsk, the seat of Kolchak's White government, was swift, and the Cossack Hetman Annenkov was immediately dispatched to quell the uprising. His forces arrived by train on 8 September, stopping about six kilometres from Slavgorod, near Arkhangelsk, where they plundered and burned the village. Two days later they recaptured Slavgorod. Four hundred peasants were killed in the battle for the city, and another 2,000 were killed in the ensuing punitive raids on the surrounding villages, including Podsosnovo.[12]

These events make only cameo appearances in Tina Hinz's memoir. Tina describes the years of the civil war as difficult but offers few details. She seems to conflate a number of different civil war events with the dramatic peasant uprising near her home. She notes that both the Red and the White Armies exchanged their tired horses for fresh mounts, which they confiscated from the villagers in Nikolaipol. In general, she describes the White Army as being more brutal to the resident population. The Whites sometimes shot people on the street at random, and she reports that they took two young men from Nikolaipol with them who were never heard from again. The events of the peasant uprising and their consequences for Podsosnovo left a distinct impression on Tina in that they "were remembered for a long time." She recalls the battle and how "the rumbling went on for hours before it finally became quiet."[13] Here her memory again combines events. The peasant uprising culminates with a Red Army victory rather than the punitive actions of the White Army Cossacks. Her handwritten version and the version published by her family in Germany illustrate the subtleties of social context in the telling of stories. In her memoir, Tina claims "our side won, the Whites had to flee," while in her family's edited version the same passage proclaims "the Reds won, the Whites had to flee." Her version told in the 1960s and that of her descendants in Germany in the 1990s tell the story in ways that were politically and socially acceptable for their respective contexts.

The events of the civil war and the clash of peasants and Cossacks in a village nearby seem not to have touched the extended Werner family directly. The events of the summer of 1921, however, would devastate them. Tina's memoir tells the story of the loss of Ivan's father and grandfather with much greater detail than my father could have remembered or possibly ever knew. Tina begins her account by capturing the intense sense of foreboding she had on a Monday or Tuesday. Her father and brother Johann had been threshing and came home dusty, tired, and hungry. They had a sense of satisfaction, however, because they reported that the crop was now completely under roof. Tina was weepy and told them she sensed someone was going to die or something important was about to happen. Her brothers and father tenderly tried to reassure and encourage her. Her mother and other women in the family do not enter the account, possibly because her mother was recovering from typhus and might not have been up and about. Her husband Jakob finally suggested they go home to sleep, and the others agreed that "tomorrow things will be better."[14]

Shortly after going to sleep, according to her account, Tina woke up not feeling well and "had to go out to vomit, had diarrhea, and had to vomit again and again. It did not stop anymore." She did not return to the bedroom, where her husband was asleep, until morning, when he realized how sick she was and scolded her for not saying anything to him earlier. He put her back to bed and covered her with a blanket. Soon she began to have cramps in her legs, and then the cramps moved up her body until she also had severe stomach cramps. Jakob ran to get her father, who suggested she be given no water to drink, only peppermint tea. She recalls that she could not see her father because her "eyes had sunk too far into [her] head." As the disease progressed, she developed even more intense abdominal pain and shortness of breath. She remembers little of the next days; however, in an apparently delirious state, she gave birth to twin boys on Saturday of that week. The twins were stillborn.

The symptoms Tina describes are those of cholera, a disease caused by a bacterium ingested from contaminated food or drinking water. The disease strikes quickly and if not treated can cause death within hours. The epidemic that gripped the village of Nikolaipol would eventually spare Tina but claim many lives among the extended Werner family and in the rest of the village. According to her account, Peter Born from the village had fallen ill on Tuesday at four o'clock and was dead by midnight. On Wednesday evening, her father Johann had become ill. Her brother Johann, my grandfather, had gone to the mill with her sister Maria's husband that day, and both had returned home deathly ill. Father and son had died that same Wednesday night, 26 August 1921, and the younger Johann had been buried in the same coffin with his father. Maria lost her husband and two daughters, but she recovered. My grandmother Anna survived, as did her son Hans, my father, but his sister Anna did not.[15] Abram, the last surviving adult male Werner family member, became ill and died on Saturday of that week. In total, the village lost thirty-five people to the cholera epidemic. A combined funeral service was held for them at the school, but many family members were too weak physically and emotionally to attend. Tina candidly remarks it was simply "too much at once."[16]

Tina (Werner) Hinz's memoir follows the model described by Jill Ker Conway, who suggests that, for women writers to convince their readers to "take up an important cause" or "follow a new spiritual path," as Hinz does, they cannot depart too far from "accepted stereotypes which affirm the man of action and the suffering or redemptive female."[17] Hinz is clear about the purpose for writing down her story: "I wish to write down as well as I can my life experiences so that, if after a long time my children think of reading them, they may come to know what my life here on earth was, and as a result they will learn to know me better." She is conscious that her memories—the intimate—will become public even if only for her extended family. Hinz clearly wants the memoir to be read as an exhortation for her children to maintain the Christian faith. She becomes explicit about this purpose at the end of the memoir, where she assures her readers that, based on her experiences, "when the storms of life come and the strongest can hardly stand," holding on to faith is the only way of surviving.[18] Certainly her depiction of her growing-up years follows the pattern of painting her father and brothers in a heroic fashion. She portrays them as sensitive men of action making good on the Siberian plain. In the second part of the memoir, where she chronicles her later life and where the story of my father's family does not reappear, men are subsumed into the evil forces that conspire to separate Hinz from her God. Her memoir focuses on her suffering, and though she becomes a revered midwife in this latter part of her story, the dominant theme of her memoir is her suffering.

The memoir is dated February 1968, and it appears that all but the last few pages were written at that time. The timing coincided with her seventieth year and a temporary lull in the repression of religion. The strong anti-religious tone of the Khruschev era ended with his removal in 1964, and, though the state remained anti-religious, in the first years of the Brezhnev era anti-religious policies were pursued less aggressively than they had been before and would be thereafter.[19] The memoir is written from the vantage point of a deeply religious woman who experienced trauma and incredible sadness. She casts her story as one in which God determined a difficult path for her yet one she still believes was all for her good. The story has a significant turning point that comes when her entry into adulthood coincides with events of history—revolution, war, hunger, and repression. The memories of her childhood paint a picture of an idyllic life. The memories of later years of tragedy seem to enhance these memories of childhood, a childhood that flowed by quickly but was peaceful and beautiful.

Hinz also tells her story using models typical of Soviet German diasporic narratives. The essential themes of this narrative paint the period after 1917 as a time of troubles that ended a golden age for Germans in Russia. They had been secure in their sense of identity as a German-speaking minority; their institutions, churches, and families had all contributed to a sense of confidence in and even the superiority of their culture. After these events, the tone of the memoir reflects a sense of personal and group loss. The waves of revolution, civil war, famine, arrest, exile, and the Second World War washed over them in rapid succession, and they came to see their lives as those of a repressed minority at the mercy of a heartless regime. Even though their ancestors had left German lands in the eighteenth century, they would increasingly come to see their homeland as Germany, where they believed the ideal ethnic past could be re-created. Hinz did not live to see the diasporic imagination become reality with the migrations to Germany that took place in the 1990s. Her memoir conveys to some extent, however, the mentality that would give energy to the mass migrations of Soviet Germans to Germany after the fall of the Berlin Wall.[20]

For my father, the missing history of his family allowed him to speculate about his origin. The appearance of Hinz's memoir rendered his speculative stories of origin obsolete. Listening to an account of his family history before a time he could remember proved somewhat disconcerting. He found it difficult to say much about the story—it was a strange tale to him. Even though the memoirist was someone whom he clearly remembered visiting, he could not identify with her narrative of his family's origins. The emergence of this competing story illustrated most clearly a pattern in his storytelling. He generally trusted only his own memory and versions of stories. Although he could not discount this version, he also could not make it his own.

PART 2

War

War Stories

THE TRAIN THAT PICKED UP IVAN and his fellow recruits in the fall of 1938 unloaded them at a military installation in Kirov, where he began basic training. It meant first of all stripping and putting all of one's personal belongings into a bag that was taken away to be put in storage "somewhere." Next was the mandatory shower and haircut, followed by the donning of the uniform and the march back to the barracks, which completed the transformation to military life. During basic training, Ivan occasionally crossed paths with Martens and Kroeker, the two local boys with whom he had been drafted, but otherwise was only vaguely aware that young men from other German-speaking villages had also been drafted. Clearly the stories of becoming a soldier, basic training, and eventual assignment to a mechanized unit made little lasting impressions on my father, since he only recalled these events when I formally prompted him in a taped interview.

His experience with equipment as a member of the MTS meant that Ivan was a desirable candidate for the mechanized units of the army, and after basic training he was assigned to a tank unit. It also meant that he lost track of his village friends and never crossed paths with other Mennonites or Siberian Germans again. Becoming part of a tank unit meant a change of location to Chelyabinsk in the Ural Mountains, where the mandatory six months of basic training he received at Kirov were supplemented with a few months of tank training. He was trained as a tank driver, a task that required both driving and mechanical skills. The summer of 1939 must have been uneventful from his point of view; there were no stories of new friends made, camaraderie, antics, or other noteworthy happenings. The outbreak of the Second World War when the German Army attacked Poland in September 1939 was also not an event of which my father had a personal memory.

His first war stories began in the winter of 1940 during the Winter War between the Soviet Union and Finland. On 30 November 1939, the giant Soviet Union attacked Finland after Stalin tried unsuccessfully to gain territory from the Finns by negotiation. The Finnish border was on the outskirts of Leningrad; the Finns had offered a smaller buffer than Stalin had asked for, and ultimately he had decided to attack the much smaller Finland. The war went badly for the Red Army. Although vastly superior in numbers, the Red Army faced determined Finnish soldiers fighting on home ground. My father always maintained that the Soviets initially sent their southern troops into battle in the snow, soldiers who really did not know what winter was. To some extent, this was true. The Soviets sent regional troops dressed in brown uniforms and boots in winter to fight against Finnish troops on skis and dressed in white.[1]

Ivan became part of the Winter War later, when the Red Army launched a massive offensive in February 1940 to break through the Mannerheim Line, a goal that had eluded it in the months after the initial attack. My father's story always began with a strange event that was difficult to picture from his description. Ivan's unit was entrained in Chelyabinsk and then travelled to Moscow, where they were all taken to some kind of theatre. In the taped interview of these events, my father described it as "a big show—the whole train stopped, there were many train runs, about three or four every day. We all got into the Moscow city theatre, thousands of people could get into the theatre; there they showed us live tanks; they had a turntable stage, where they tried to show us the way the war actually was."[2]

My father's memories were unclear about the dates for the unit's transfer to the Karelian Isthmus. Accounts of the Winter War indicate that a Soviet troop build-up in the weeks before signalled a massive assault on the Mannerheim Line that began on 11 February 1940.[3] To defend against the Soviet attack, Finnish troops had concentrated their limited resources where they would be most effective. The railway line from Leningrad to Finland represented the only effective way for Soviet troops to enter the theatre of war, and one of my father's most vivid memories was of the train being shelled even before it could be unloaded.

We went into the bush and were already being fired upon by the artillery. We went by rail past Leningrad, and the railway went right into Finland. We unloaded the tanks off of the rail cars, and most of the rail cars tipped. We just turned the tank on the flat car and drove it off into the snow; it was very rough. We didn't fool around with unloading. Some of the tanks were broken right there; they tore off their tracks while unloading. There was just snow, brush, and stones; you couldn't see where you were, you just drove off the train. You just turned around right on the train car and drove off, and the tank was so heavy the train car tipped. You just took off, the train cars didn't roll very far, they just stayed there. The train could not travel any further; it just stayed there and had to be fixed before it could move.[4]

I asked my father how he had felt during this first taste of coming under fire. He had little to say other than there were no words to describe how one felt in these circumstances. Other than the images of their arrival on the front, my father had no specific stories about the main battles of the Winter War. He generally indicated that the fighting had been fierce in the first days of the assault, that they had made progress, and that after a week or so they had begun to move forward with less resistance. My brothers recall him mentioning the danger posed by Molotov cocktails, bottles filled with gasoline that were lit before being dropped into a tank's air intake, causing a fire and forcing the tank crew out of the machine, where they came under infantry fire and certain death. My father told stories of Finnish soldiers joining Red Army food kitchens for a meal, and of deadly accurate Finnish women snipers, but these stories did not seem to have been his experiences. They might well have circulated among the Soviet troops as front-line stories.

Military histories of the Winter War provide some context for Ivan's experiences. For this war, the Red Army's tanks were organized into brigades under the command of infantry divisions. Based on my father's stories, it is likely that he was in one of the five tank brigades attached to the 123rd Rifle Division, part of the 7th Army. The division broke through the Mannerheim Line on 11 February 1940 near the village of Summa.[5] The massive assault began with an intense bombardment of the line by Soviet artillery. The military strategists having learned from earlier mistakes, now had the infantry accompany the tanks. The tanks moved forward in a leapfrog fashion with the infantry moving with them to consolidate the ground gained. Descriptions of the destruction of the bunkers of the Mannerheïm Line note the key role of tank drivers in manoeuvring their machines to give protection to the infantry from the machine guns inside them.

In contrast to the nebulous accounts of the assault on the Mannerheim Line, my father's memories of being wounded were vivid and clear. Sometime around 8 March 1940, Ivan's tank brigade was advancing along the road to the Finnish city of Vipurii when Ivan drove over a mine that blew the track off the tank's sprockets. His tank had to stop while the infantry carried on. He and another crew member got out to fix the track using spare links he had with him. His helper crawled back into the tank ahead of him, and as Ivan was getting into the tank "someone fired out of a house nearby—with a machine gun—and he hit me in the leg. Actually he hit the tank, and the bullet ricocheted, so it hit the tank and then went into my leg at a slant and fairly deeply. I did not notice it—I jumped in, started up, and drove off, and after having driven for a while I noticed that the leg was always falling asleep. I felt my leg, and my pants were all bloody, and then I realized I was wounded."[6]

The tank crew put out a white flag with a red cross on it, and an armoured vehicle came to pick Ivan up. It was driven a few kilometres away from the front, and Ivan and other wounded soldiers were transferred to a heated truck, which drove them to Leningrad. While he was in the hospital, the war in Finland ended, and Ivan recalled watching the victory parade on the streets of Leningrad from his hospital window. An officer of his unit also came to visit him, and he received a medal or citation of some kind.[7] It was never clear what he received it for, but there were many medals and awards granted during the Winter War to boost morale. For instance, 237 men from the 35th Light Tank Brigade, which fought with the 123rd Rifle Division in the breakthrough of the Mannerheim Line, received medals of various kinds.[8] Ivan might have been one of them. Although my father could not remember specifically, he thought he had spent about two months in the hospital, in part because the wound had become infected and in part because he had required considerable physiotherapy even after the wound had healed.

The wounding in Finland and his recovery seem to have marked a turning point in how Ivan felt about his past life in Siberia, including the relationship with his wife. Since my father never told stories about his first marriage, this turning point is less clear and can only be inferred. With his hospital stay coming to an end in late spring of 1940, Ivan was given leave. Finally, one would think, there was an opportunity to see his family and wife Anna again after having been away for almost two years. But he did not go home. When asked why, my father explained that the leave was only two weeks, and it would have taken all of the two weeks—in fact two weeks would not have been enough time—to get to Siberia and back. Sharing a hospital room with him in Leningrad was an infantry soldier named Buki, who came from Georgia near the city of Tbilisi. Buki invited—begged—Ivan to join him at his home in Georgia when they obtained their leaves at the same time. The trip to and from Georgia, according to my father, took only a total of six days, leaving them a week in the warmer Caucasian climate. Buki thought Ivan would get along well with his family and explained that Georgians liked Germans. His sister was a schoolteacher who spoke fluent German, and Buki assured Ivan that he could converse with her in German while the two of them would speak Russian to each other, quietly, because Georgians hated Russians. Ivan agreed, and the two of them took the train to Tbilisi, where he spent a week with Buki's family. It was a beautiful area where they grew grapes, and my father's accounts of staying there were told with fondness. My father recounted how Buki coached him to speak only German when a Cherkessian wearing his ancient warrior dress, complete with a sword, entered the restaurant where Ivan was dining with Buki, his sister, and some friends. The Cherkessian went by and patted him on the back and assured him that Georgians liked Germans.[9]

When Ivan returned to active duty, he was assigned to a unit whose summer camp was near Velikiye Luki, about 450 kilometres west of Moscow. The spring months seem to have been a relatively quiet time for the unit. My father described in some detail the summer lodgings they made out of shingles cut from the trunks of trees in the dense evergreen forest near a river where they were encamped, but otherwise time passed by uneventfully until mid-June.

The two giants of totalitarianism were not idle, however. As part of the Ribbentrop–Molotov Non-Aggression Pact signed by Germany and the Soviet Union in 1939, the smaller states of Eastern Europe were divided between Stalin and Hitler to be incorporated into their growing empires. In mid-June 1940, Stalin delivered an ultimatum to the Baltic states of Lithuania, Latvia, and Estonia effectively forcing them to surrender their sovereignty. With the rest of the world preoccupied with Hitler's attack on

France, the Baltic states had no option but to capitulate. The relatively relax-
ing spring in the forest was interrupted by these events, which my father
remembered clearly.

Beginning on 16 June, the Red Army suddenly occupied the three Baltic
countries of Lithuania, Latvia, and Estonia. A few days before the invasion,
without any explanation, Ivan's unit received instructions in manners and
decorum. They were issued a supply of cigarettes and matches with specific
instructions to use their own matches to light cigarettes rather than borrow
a light from the glowing cigarette of a fellow soldier. The cigarettes were an
unaccustomed luxury compared with the tobacco and paper they usually used
to "roll your own." Ivan, now a junior officer, was issued a new white collar,
which he and the other officers who received such collars had to sew into their
uniforms. One morning at four the alarm sounded for the unit to assemble on
the nearby road, the tanks lined up one behind the other. Even junior officers
still did not know what was going on. Upon receiving the signal, the convoy
of tanks rolled forward toward the Latvian border. My father remembered
the trip being about half an hour to the frontier and another few hours to
Riga, the capital of Latvia. His account must have telescoped the time somewhat, unless their summer camp was some distance west of Velikiye Luki.
The town is some 150 kilometres from the Latvian border and about 400
kilometres from Riga. In Riga, they assisted in disarming the Latvian troops,
who received two days of rations and train tickets to go home. The rifles of the
Latvian Army were collected in a pile, and kiosks were set up where Soviet
officers issued the train tickets. A reporter for the *Chicago Tribune* who was
in Riga at the time reported that on 17 June "there was a mob at the railway
station, waving red rags and screaming in hysterical joy about the arrival of the
Russians. The Latvian language could not be heard. The speeches, the shouts,
the screams were all in Russian or Yiddish." Some tanks were even showered
with flowers.[10]

Ivan's unit remained in Riga for a month, and my father had pleasant
memories of his stay there. He "looked at the ocean, went visiting, got to
know some of the people." They had strict orders not to venture out alone,
only in twos or threes. They were also to be polite when dealing with the local
populace and were not supposed to discuss politics with anyone or provide any
information regarding their unit or any other military details. His recollections of Riga in the summer of 1940 were also one of the few occasions when

my father mentioned a friend. Petrov Krushinski was a Ukrainian with whom Ivan spent a great deal of time. Krushinski sang Ukrainian songs, which Ivan had difficulty understanding and made him laugh. His friend taught him some of them, such as "Rozpryahayte Khloptsi Koney," a popular Ukrainian folk song. On one occasion, Ivan and Petrov were walking along the ocean when they heard two young women walking behind them speaking German. In late 1939, Hitler had offered most Germans in Latvia the option of being resettled in the Warthegau—the area of occupied Poland that Hitler wanted to make a permanent German state. Most Germans had left, but some had decided to stay in their homes in the Baltics, a decision most would regret after the Soviet occupation. After making Petrov promise he would keep it secret, Ivan struck up a conversation with the women, who were shocked to meet a German-speaking Red Army soldier. They invited the two soldiers to join them for lemonade in a restaurant, and as my father recalled "we visited with them for a while; they were very nice, happy."[11]

The brief accounts of his convalescent leave in Tbilisi and the interaction with the young women on the shores of the Baltic Sea at Riga suggest that Ivan's connection to his wife and former life in Siberia was becoming less and less real. When I asked my father whether he ever got letters from home, he indicated he had received letters in the first years. He recalled the last letter he had received was about the time he had left the Leningrad hospital, though he qualified this memory by saying the letter had followed him, and he had read it only in the spring of 1941 when he was stationed at Grodno. The letters from home had seemingly not been very meaningful since there was so much the censors would not allow. Apparently the letters had only indicated that the family had enough to live on and that conditions were tolerable.

The 1940–41 winter camp for Ivan's unit was near Minsk and was the scene of one of my father's favourite stories. It was to some extent a story my father told to boast about his prowess as a young man. When he told the story, it was unconnected to time or place, and only systematic placement of his stories in a time sequence suggests that it must have taken place in the winter of 1940–41. Ivan took part in a biathlon-like competition among various units of the Red Army stationed in the area. The contest pitted the tank division against an infantry division in a fifty-kilometre race. The race involved carrying a machine gun with a supply of ammunition to a point, firing at a target, and then skiing back to the starting line. With considerable pride, my father recalled how he had come in "second by half a ski length. If I had seen him sooner, I could have passed him, I had enough energy. I thought I was alone; all of a sudden I saw someone struggling ahead of me. I caught up to him, but I was still a little behind him going through the gate."[12]

A significant turn in Ivan's perception of his role in the Soviet system also seems to have occurred sometime during the interlude between his participation in the Winter War in 1940 and the attack by Nazi Germany in June 1941. It came in connection with his desire to be a Red Army fighter pilot. Ever since his school days and the experience of glider flying, airplanes had fascinated Ivan. As my father described it, in the Red Army there was always an opportunity to advance—to try something else. Ivan seems to have taken the initiative to be transferred from a tank unit to a fighter aircraft unit. He discussed the prospects for this ambition with his senior officers, who suggested he apply. It meant appearing before a "commission," as my father called it, to be examined. Here his certificate that he had participated in a glider club as a youth stood him in good stead. He had to pass the health exam, and his educational record was reviewed. Ivan was deemed to be qualified and was transferred to the Minsk military airfield, where he began his training with the mechanical aspects of an airplane, subject matter he found easy. He spent a few weeks in the engine shop and a few more in the airframe section. Then followed a week of parachute training, and finally training in an actual airplane began. The first task was to find out if the new pilot candidate had the "stomach" for fighter aircraft manoeuvres. Ivan was put through all the loops, rolls, and turns the instructor and airplane were capable of to determine whether nausea or fear would get the better of him. When they returned to the tarmac, a doctor was there to check his health again. My father told this part of the story in a heroic fashion—none of it had bothered him—he had passed all of these tests with flying colours.

But then came the political test, which in his words "was the most important area for a pilot; then all of a sudden they called me into the office and said I could not train as a pilot because I had relatives in Canada." The Soviet regime believed that there was a heightened risk of pilots using their airplanes to defect by flying over the border and since he had family outside of the Soviet Union, he would be a security risk. He was done. After a month of further training as a mechanic, Ivan returned to his tank unit. His rejection as a prospective fighter pilot for political reasons, even though in his eyes he

Mladshiy Leytenant Ivan Ivanevich Werner in a photo likely taken at the time he became an officer. He is wearing the Budenovka, a distinctive winter hat named after a famous Russian General and still part of the Red Army uniform during the Winter War, but largely phased out by 1941. Ivan sent the photo to his family in Siberia where his sister preserved it. The photo shows evidence of frequent reproduction and this version is from a reproduction that was airbrushed in colour.

had excelled in all the other areas, was bitterly disappointing and changed his attitude. As my father put it in an interview forty-five years later, "up to that time I had always felt like a full-fledged Russian citizen, but then I started to doubt." With the benefit of later memories of the Soviet–German war, he also suggested that it had brought to mind "what my mother always said to me, that if I was in a war and had the opportunity I should rather allow myself to be captured than to be shot."[13]

It was always unclear when and in what context Ivan's promotion to the officer ranks came. Now a combat-hardened "veteran" at age twenty-three or twenty-four, Ivan was promoted to the rank of junior lieutenant that brought with it pay—170 rubles a month. My father had no specific memories, at least not ones he ever told, of why or how this happened. His revelation that he had become an officer was almost accidental and came as part of later stories of his Soviet Red Army experiences. It is clear, however, that the promotion to a junior officer occurred as part of a general reorganization and refitting of the Red Army prompted by the disastrous war against Finland. The army was reorganized, with tank divisions grouped into mechanized corps.

The tank Ivan drove during the Winter War was likely a *B7* or *T-26,* both early designs of fairly light tanks destroyed in large numbers during the war. Sometime in June 1940, while still stationed at Minsk, his unit received the first of the *T-34* tanks that would become famous during the Soviet–German battles of 1943 and 1944. Ivan's new role was to train recruits in the operation of the *T-34.* A *T-34* tank had a crew of four: a driver who sat in the lower left side of the tank, where he had a small slit to see where he was going; a machine gunner who sat in the right hand side of the tank; a commander in the turret who was also the main gunner; and a crew member in the turret whose task was to load the gun. One of the deficiencies of the Soviet tank forces was the lack of communication between tanks and between crew members within tanks, where only the commander and driver could communicate using an internal radio. The driver's task was to manoeuvre the tank as per directions from the commander, who tried to coordinate the position of the tank and its rotating turret so that it could fire at intended targets. It was like driving a car without a rear-view mirror, no side windows, and the smallest windshield imaginable.

Ivan was assigned a group of eight trainees who spent part of their time in the classroom and part of their time in the field learning how to drive the *T-34* tank. Ivan was their instructor for the hands-on training in the field. The training continued when the unit was moved to Grodno, a Polish city just inside the Soviet Union on the Soviet–German border as it had been established after the German occupation of Poland. Reorganization of the tank troops meant that Ivan's unit was now the 29th Tank Division of the 11th Mechanized Corps of the 3rd Army. Although my father had no memory of unit designations, his clear memory that they were stationed right in the city of Grodno suggests that he was assigned to the 29th Tank Division, since it was the only tank unit stationed in Grodno in the summer of 1941.[14]

Grodno was only a few kilometres away from the Soviet–German frontier, and up to 22 June 1941 the provisions of the Ribbentrop-Molotov Pact meant that the two countries were on friendly terms. There were signs, however, that all was not well. Ivan had become friends with a senior officer with whom he had served in the Winter War and who had discovered that he spoke German. The senior officer had been a German prisoner of war in the First World War and had learned to speak some German. The two of them often went for a walk in the woods near Grodno, where the senior officer took the opportunity to practise his German. On one of these walks, he told Ivan that ethnic Germans were being released from active military service and ostensibly were being sent home. He indicated to Ivan that they were not in fact going home but being put into work battalions as virtual slave labour building defence works. The senior officer indicated to Ivan that he had intervened and that Ivan would not be released to suffer the same fate.

Formal recognition of his knowledge of German meant that Ivan now served in a semi-official capacity as a translator for his unit. Occasionally, and according to my father's recollection right up to the days before the attack, German officers paid visits to their Russian counterparts, and my father recalled two occasions when he was invited to translate. On one of these visits, officers from the two sides watched a Soviet film about the famous Soviet aviator, Valery Chkalov. Chkalov was a hero of the Soviet Union in part because of his long-distance flight over the North Pole to the United States.[15] My father's memories of this movie seemed to be out of proportion to its importance in his overall story. It might have been his lifelong interest in flying that heightened his retention of the details of the movie. My father recalled the details of the life of the young and mischievous Chkalov and the constant trouble he was in. He remembered how the film portrayed the dashing Chkalov flying between the water and a bridge when he caught sight of his girlfriend on it. While the film was being shown, a German officer leaned over to Ivan and assured him that the Germans also had good pilots. They took the German officers home at about eleven o'clock, and in his recollection the war with Germany began early the next morning.[16]

Seldom are we more curious about individual memories than when a person has participated in dramatic and often "historical" events such as wars. Undoubtedly, for most people who made my father's acquaintance, they would remember most consistently his war stories. In fact, for years they were almost the only stories he told and the only material he had available to hold a conversation of any length. There was little deviation in the narrative structure or details of the stories. As the oldest son, I heard his stories from the time I was old enough to comprehend them until he died when I was fifty, a period of forty or more years. I also interviewed him formally, and throughout all his accounts of war experiences his stories seldom strayed from their scripts. Oral historian Alice Hoffman and others suggest that our memories of the past are scripted: that is, events "are assessed at the time they occur, or shortly thereafter, as salient and hence important to remember." These events are then "rehearsed or otherwise consolidated" to become part of lasting long-term memory and are usually told in the same way time and again.[17]

Listening to the stories of his first combat experiences in the Finnish war, it was always unclear to me why my father had no specific memories of what must have been tension-filled and emotional weeks for a twenty-two-year-old man experiencing combat for the first time. Hoffman's analysis of her husband's memories suggests there is a "primacy" effect in the preservation of war memories. The first occurrence of a life-threatening event, in this case the shelling while still on the train, is often the only one retained in memory even

Map 3. Places where Ivan was stationed as a Red Army soldier.

though subsequent events might have been equally dramatic and dangerous.[18] It might be, however, that my father never had an audience to whom it was possible to tell stories of his direct participation in the killing of others. He was not likely to tell such stories in my presence when I was a boy. In most of his war stories, something was done to him rather than vice versa. In the context of the pacifist Mennonite social milieu in which he told his stories, accounts of his direct participation in killing might well have been untenable.

It is also apparent from my father's stories that his draft into the Red Army began a steady mental and emotional separation from his life in Siberia. A number of turning points marked this separation. The decision to join his friend in Georgia when my father went on leave, the stories that suggest renewed interest in meeting women, and hence the emotional detachment from his wife Anna all point to a new orientation. His rejection for training as a fighter pilot seems to have been the first serious challenge to his sense of being able to thrive under the Stalinist system of the Soviet Union. In hindsight, he marked that event as having paved the way for his reaction to capture by the Germans.

6

Johann: Becoming a German

At three in the morning on 22 June 1941, all hell broke loose. Ivan awoke to a tremendous crash. The air was choked with dust. The barracks where he slept had suffered a direct hit by bombs. Those soldiers who could ran outside, where they were greeted by a terrible scene in the early morning light. The military compound, which also had a tent city of troops, was a mass of confusion and death. As the sky brightened, the air filled with German Stuka dive-bombers. Wave after wave of Stukas tipped their noses into a dive. The siren mounted on the airplane's belly began to scream as the plane picked up speed and grew in intensity until it released its deadly cargo and broke off its dive. Ivan ran to the garage to his tank, which was always fuelled up at the end of each day's training, and began manoeuvring through the confused troops to the previously determined assembly point outside the city. He needed to cross the Neman River, but the bridge had already been bombed. He was finally able to cross at an emergency bridge, which brought him to the assembly point in a young forest. Here confusion also reigned. One high-ranking officer rode by on his horse dressed only in his underwear and barking out meaningless orders. Ivan simply advised the officer that there was no way of recognizing him without a uniform. He only seemed to realize then that he had no clothes on. The German artillery could be heard firing in the distance, with each volley coming closer to the forest, now teeming with confused soldiers, tanks, guns, and trucks. The air was full of Stukas. Hiding was almost impossible. Inexperienced soldiers ran out into the open screaming like wild animals, and the airplanes came and mowed them down with their wing-mounted machine guns. Rather than finding even a small bush or hollow to hide behind, they just ran right out into the open. Ivan hid his tank as best he could and crept under its sloping protective armour each time a wave of Stukas descended on their position.

Operation Barbarossa, as Hitler had named the attack on the Soviet Union, had initially been planned to begin in May but had been delayed because the German army had to assist the Italians in the campaign in Crete. In the weeks before 22 June, there had been a steady build-up of German forces on the border with the Soviet Union. Slowly, over three million soldiers, more than 7,000 guns, and 3,350 tanks inched their way into position during the nights before the massive attack was launched.[1]

It took hours that Sunday before any semblance of organization returned to the Red Army or orders arrived to deal with the German attack. It would take until 9:15 p.m. before General Timoshenko's order for the Soviet armies to attack the invaders arrived at the front. Local commanders were left to their own initiatives, and by 10:00 a.m. the commander of the 11th Mechanized Corps had committed the 29th Tank Division to a counterattack.[2] The confusion, however, had disrupted everything, and Ivan took his tank into battle with a crew of recruits who had been trained on anti-tank weapons but had never fired a tank gun. He also became the tank's commander since there was no one to assume that role. That meant the tank essentially had no main gunner, not as big a problem as it might have been because they were also terribly short of ammunition since the Germans seemed to know where all the ammunition dumps were and systematically blew them up. As a result, Ivan's tank was issued only five shells for the counterattack. The division, which had assembled southeast of Grodno, was to counterattack in a northwesterly direction together with the other tank division of the corps and its infantry division. Both of these units, however, were some distance away and in an even worse state of organization.

The 29th Tank Division counterattacked alone, and, though it was later described as one of the more successful Soviet attempts to stem the German tide, it managed only to push the attacker back seven or eight kilometres.[3] The division and the rest of the 11th Mechanized Corps did not last long. An operational report on the evening of 22 June suggested the unit was still fighting at 3:45 p.m., had withdrawn by 5:00 p.m., and by the next morning had seemingly disappeared. The headquarters of the 3rd Army had no information on their whereabouts. In my father's accounts, the counterattack was almost useless. With little ammunition and an inexperienced crew, his tank was soon ineffective, and Ivan retreated to try to get fuel and ammunition. He recalled stops in Lida and Baranavichy, two towns east of Grodno, to try to get ammunition.[4]

There were tragedies all around, and Ivan was in the middle of them. In a story not part of my father's usual repertoire, a Ukrainian soldier in Ivan's unit named Kulakov, who in his story spoke Mennonite Low German, was struck in the neck by a bullet as the two of them were crossing a road. Ivan assured Kulakov he would be all right as he held him and tried to stop the bleeding. Kulakov died in his arms. In another story, an officer asked Ivan to transport his family to the rear. Although families were to be evacuated on transport trucks, all available vehicles were clogged with people. Since they had less than the normal four-man complement, there was some room, but having the woman and her two young children in the tank complicated everything. The added burden of trying to assure their safety in a war zone added tremendously to the already stressful situation.

On the morning of 23 June, the crew attempted to drive their tank to Minsk, but by noon they were forced into hiding because of the unending attacks from airplanes. They stopped in a wood, and the woman and her two children decided to walk to a nearby village to get food and supplies. Ivan and his tank crew hid the tank as best they could and waited for nightfall to continue their retreat. By evening, the woman and her children had not returned, and together with an officer from another tank crew they set off to the village to find her. Before reaching the village, they came upon the family. The mother had been shot, likely by strafing airplanes—she was dead. Her two children were at her side crying and begging for their mother. There was nothing left to do but bury the woman and attempt to find someone to care for the children. The other officer went into the village and managed to find a family to take the two children.

There was little time to appreciate or think about the horror of the scene. Night was falling, and there was evidence all around them that the attacking Germans were steadily advancing and that they were in danger of being surrounded. The only way out was toward Minsk. Ivan and his crew managed to find some fuel and set off to drive east through the night. By this time, travelling on the roads was almost impossible. There were burned-out and abandoned vehicles everywhere. One could not drive on the road for even a

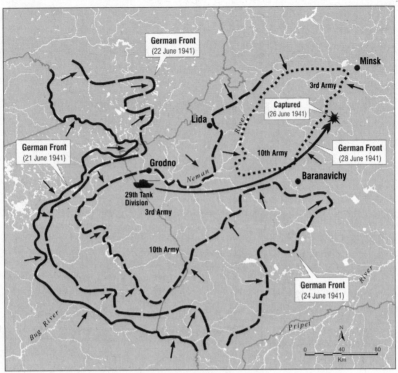

Map 4. German attack on the Soviet Union, June 1941.

hundred metres. Ivan had to drive the tank in the ditch because the road was
filled with dead horses, abandoned cannons, vehicles, and people trying to
escape from the front. They tried to travel during the day but made only about
twenty kilometres before a bomb from a Stuka fell near them, spraying their
tank with dirt and gravel. Some stones lodged in the tracks, and they "played
dead" until nightfall before prying the stones out so they could continue. They
were only able to travel by night, and finding fuel and food became an overriding problem. When they caught a whiff of what smelled like roasting bread,
they and everyone else in the vicinity descended on what was left of a burning bread truck. In the fray, Ivan managed to get only one bag of bread, and
it was so hard it could not be bitten into. The crew reasoned that, if they saw
frogs in the puddles in the ditches beside the road, the water could not be too
unhealthy. They brushed aside the slime and dipped the bread into the water
so they could eat it. During the night, likely the night of 25 June, they ran out
of fuel and were forced to sit in the open in plain sight of German airplanes.

In the early dawn hours of 26 June, they peered out of their tank anxiously, watching the sky for airplanes. Suddenly they saw soldiers in the forest a short distance away. In my father's recollection, there were about twenty of them in black uniforms with a skull and crossbones on their foreheads. Although this suggests they were members of the Totenkopf Division, the feared Death's Head division of the Waffen SS, there were no Totenkopf Division units in the area in 1941. The black uniforms likely belonged to regular Panzer troops mopping up what had become a huge encirclement of three Soviet armies.

At first, Ivan's crew thought the figures emerging from the forest were fellow Soviet soldiers, and they were going to get out of the tank to try to get help to continue. Ivan cautioned his inexperienced crew that the Soviet Red Army had no armed units that he knew of with black uniforms. As they approached, Ivan heard the unmistakable sound of German, the language of his childhood and that of his personal thoughts. When he thought he heard discussions among the soldiers about blowing up his tank, he made a quick decision to surrender, a decision suggested to him by his mother before he left Siberia. Stalin's soldiers were not to surrender. According to my father, they all knew surrender meant instant execution if the long tentacles of Stalin's iron grip ever caught them.[5]

Ivan jumped out through his hatch and rolled into the ditch nearby, landing right near a German soldier, who was too surprised to fire his weapon. He calmed down when Ivan began to speak to him in German. The soldier could not come to terms with what confronted him. "Are you a German spy in a Russian tank?" he asked. Ivan explained that he was a German from Russia. The German called to the others, explaining that they had captured a German. The group decided that he should call for the others to get out of the tank, which he did. They were taken away as prisoners of war, while Ivan was taken to the unit's command post. It was only about two kilometres from where they had run out of fuel during the night. His first interview with the officer in charge was brief. The officer assured him he would not be treated like a prisoner because they were not fighting against other Germans. The exhaustion and tension of the last few days caught up to Ivan, and he went to sleep.

After he slept, Ivan was interviewed about his background, and when he mentioned the names of his neighbours in Siberia the officer noted that they were all Mennonite names and offered that his name was Derksen. Although Derksen was also a common Mennonite name, and he seemed to know about Mennonites, the officer did not admit to being Mennonite himself. The next few days were spent in a variety of tasks. Ivan had to show the Germans the features of his *T-34* tank and was called upon to interview a group of captured Soviet soldiers who claimed to be Germans. According to my father, the German military investigated his genealogy and a week or so after being captured came back with the suggestion that his grandparents had been married in East Prussia. Ivan was then transferred to the job of translating for the German Army. It captured some 350,000 Red Army soldiers in what is known as the Minsk pocket, and the logistical problems of dealing with them were overwhelming. So that he would not be confused with Red Army soldiers, Ivan was given a German uniform, though it was missing the eagle insignia, and he spent his days accompanying German soldiers who went into the large POW enclosures near Minsk to translate for them.[6]

On one foray into these enclosures, Ivan came face to face with a *politruk*. Politruks were political commissars with the same rank as an officer. A feature introduced by Trotsky during the civil war, the political commissar's role was to maintain appropriate communist vigilance in the army, and rank-and-file Red Army soldiers generally disliked politruks. According to my father, a politruk stopped him and demanded he be treated like a captured officer rather than an ordinary soldier. My father responded by asking him if he was aware that all the politruks were being shot. He advised him to remove his politruk shoulder patch, cover the area with mud so there would be no evidence of it, and keep his mouth shut about deserving better treatment. The story suggests that my father knew early about the infamous order issued by Hitler on 12 May 1941 that called for the liquidation of all political commissars.[7] The story also matched the common belief among Germans that all *Politruks* were Jews. As my father put it, "they were, I would say, 100 percent Jews, and that [fact] the Germans also knew."[8] Prisoners kept arriving at the hastily constructed enclosures, and my father remembered that, during the time he served as an interpreter, the number of POWs in the camp in which he worked rose to 48,000. He was treated like a German but could not enter the camps unless accompanied by another German soldier.

During his time as interpreter, Ivan also came across the senior officer with whom he had spoken German and who had intervened to prevent him from being sent to a work battalion. When the officer saw him, he shook his head. In a bizarre twist, Ivan suggested to the officer that he would go to his German superiors and tell them he had found another German among the POWs who was afraid to identify himself. The officer agreed and was taken out of the camp and given the job of recording the names of new POW arrivals. Ivan's role as an interpreter lasted for a week or two, after which Ivan and a group of ten other Soviet Germans were sent to occupied Poland.

In Hitler's grand *Lebensraum* scheme, an area of occupied Poland renamed Warthegau was to be cleared of its Slavic population to be resettled with the German minorities from Eastern Europe with the clear intent that it was to become a new German province. The Non-Aggression Pact signed by Stalin and Hitler in 1939 had also called for the exchange of populations, with Germans in Soviet-occupied areas of Poland being given the option of moving to the Warthegau. In 1940 and 1941, most of the Germans from eastern areas of Poland, Bessarabia, Bukovina, and the Baltics were resettled in the Warthegau.[9]

On the way to the Warthegau, the train on which Ivan and the group of ten young Soviet Germans were travelling stopped briefly at a station near Warsaw. My father could not remember exactly what they had done wrong but thought their mistake had been to flirt with Polish girls coming to the marketplace to sell apples. They had tried to communicate with them, and the girls had thrown them apples. Apparently, on a neighbouring siding, there was a train with returning SS soldiers to whom the girls had not thrown apples and who had complained to German officials about Ivan and his friends' behaviour. When they got to Lublin, the ten young men were promptly taken off the train and loaded onto a truck headed for the Lublin prison.

After stopping between two gates, they were unloaded, their personal belongings were put in bags with their names on them, and they were marched down a passageway into a cellar to cell number sixty-six. There was no explanation of why they had been incarcerated. One member of the group was a German who had been in the Polish Army when Nazi Germany and the Soviet Union had divided up Poland. He had been captured and ended up in a prison in Minsk. He was now part of their group and was being released to go home. This slightly older German, who also spoke Polish, helped them in a number of ways. In the cell was a high barred window, and they lifted Ivan up on their shoulders; he saw a beautifully landscaped inner courtyard with flowers and shrubs. In this courtyard, prisoners regularly exercised, and when they did not run fast enough their SS guards regularly whipped them. The group agreed that when it was their turn for exercise they would walk, not run, and the older German would complain to the guards that they were Germans and should not be mistreated like the other prisoners. They did this, and after some consultation the SS guards allowed them to walk in peace. One day they all had to strip and hand in their clothes, which were then laundered and brought back to them. They were escorted back to the same gated area, given back their personal belongings, and taken to the train station. There was no hint of why they had been arrested or why they were now being released. The only word they got was that they were going to Litzmannstadt (Łódź), where someone would pick them up. When they arrived at Litzmannstadt, there was a small bus—it looked quite inviting compared with their recent experience—that took them to a resettlement camp at 25 Warsaw Street in Pabianitz (Pabianice), just outside the city.[10]

Ivan's first experience of life in civilian Nazi Germany came in the camp's office, and my father's recollection of that encounter was vivid and telling. After entering the office, Ivan first saw a secretary and then the camp commander, who was "terribly fat, and then his dog lay beside him, a bulldog who looked just like him." Ivan had trouble understanding the camp commander even though he was fluent in German. He had to ask the secretary what he had said: Ivan had been told they were not to have contact with any Jewish or Polish girls, or they would be shot. Commenting on the experience some forty-five years later in Canada, my father noted that he had not been accustomed to such attitudes. He had not been "used to there being a difference between Jews and Poles and anybody else. We all concluded we would have to change considerably."[11]

When they were processed, the group of ten settled into an entire floor of a building. Their suite had shared kitchen facilities, but each had his own bedroom. Each also got a wardrobe of civilian clothes, including a sharp-looking suit. They had a food allocation and were surprised when it included strong-smelling cheese unfamiliar to them that they traded for fruit jam. Nazi ideology was intent on preserving the Germanness of minorities in Eastern Europe, and the efforts of the Reich Commission for the Strengthening of Germandom (RKFDV) and the Volksdeutsche Mittelstelle (VoMi) were dedicated to that goal. These Nazi organizations planned cultural and social events for resettled ethnic Germans to introduce them to and integrate them into Hitler's Germany.[12] My father recalled being taught social graces—such as how to behave in the presence of a German lady and learning to dance the foxtrot. At some time during the process of his socialization as a German, he also became Johann rather than Ivan.

Johann immediately applied for work at the local military airfield just outside Litzmannstadt. Probably his interest in flying contributed to that choice, and his familiarity with airplanes and qualifications as a trained mechanic helped him to get the job. The airport was about fifteen kilometres from Pabianitz, but a streetcar ride and a twenty-minute walk got him there. The airfield was a base for twin-engine bombers going to and coming back from the eastern front, and Johann was assigned a variety of tasks, including fuelling airplanes, packing the dirt runways, and replacing worn-out engines with ones rebuilt in German factories. The airport was the scene of many spectacular crashes when badly shot-up bombers returned from their missions and tried to land. Sometimes their tires were flat, and everything seemed to be going well until the weight of the airplane came down on the tires and the plane either spun around like a top or dug its nose and propellers into the ground. While Johann was there, the runway was extended after a heavily loaded bomber failed to gain sufficient altitude to clear the trees at the end of the runway and crashed and exploded.

In spring, according to my father's story, Johann decided to quit his job at the airport because of an incident in the washroom. One day he overheard a conversation in the bathroom between two pilots, who were discussing their reliance on "Russians" to repair their airplanes. "This is how far it has come," one remarked, "that the Russians have to rebuild our airplanes; I don't trust it; I don't want to fly that thing if he," meaning Johann, "has touched it." Johann immediately went to his superior and reported what he had heard. The superior demanded to know who had made the remark. Johann indicated that he had not seen the pilot's face, but in any case, if he was being suspected of sabotage, he was giving notice that he was quitting. The superior tried to convince him that it was only one "dummkopf," but Johann was not persuaded. If one pilot believed it, his influence could spread the rumour, and he refused to work under such conditions. Johann also indicated to his superior that he was German and a civilian and could not be forced to work there.[13]

His next job was driving a truck for the Carl Leib business on Breslauer Strasse in Pabianitz. The job involved loading groceries or coal for distribution in Pabianitz and towns and villages within a fifty-kilometre radius. The truck Johann drove was powered by wood or coal and had a trailer attached. He usually had two Polish workers assigned to help unload the truck at the grocery stores. The firm's owner, Carl Leib, was an officer and pilot in the Luftwaffe and was only at home briefly between missions, approximately every two

Johann seated in the truck he drove for the Carl Leib firm in Pabianitz, Poland. Posing with him are his Polish helpers. The cylinder behind the cab is the gasifier, which converted wood or coal into combustible gases.

weeks. When Johann was caught up with his grocery distribution runs, he was sometimes called upon to fill in as driver for the family.

In unrecorded stories of his later war experiences, my father made obscure references to a Mennonite woman; in one case, he referred to her as Mrs. Fast, with whom the group of friends he lived with in Pabianitz kept in correspondence after they were scattered throughout the European theatre of war. When I interviewed him formally, I asked him to clarify this story. He explained that she was a widow who had been evacuated to the Warthegau in 1942 whose maiden name had been Fast but who had been married to a Russian. Almost in the same sentence, he seemed to suggest she might not have been a widow in the sense that her Russian husband had died but in the sense that he had not accompanied her to the Warthegau—he had stayed behind in Russia. My father used the story of Mrs. Fast to explain how he knew about what had happened to some of his friends after they were separated. He closed his explanation by noting that at a certain point all contact with Mrs. Fast and his friends was lost, presumably because the Red Army occupied the area in January 1945.[14]

Work at the Carl Leib firm was interrupted by a significant event for Johann and his friends. In the fall of 1942, the travelling citizenship commissions came to Litzmannstadt to process ethnic German citizenship applications. Surviving documents from Johann's naturalization situate the events of his time in the Warthegau more firmly in a chronological sequence than my father's stories did. According to these sources, the process began on 6 October 1942, and the various file cards of the Einwandererzentralstelle (EWZ), the travelling Nazi citizenship commission that processed them, indicate that Johann had been employed at the airport and note that at the time of his being processed for citizenship his occupation was truck driver but that he was also a qualified auto mechanic for both gasoline- and diesel-powered vehicles. They note that he had a driver's licence that qualified him to drive trucks. Other documents indicate that he received his driver's licence on 7 June 1942, suggesting that his employment with the Carl Leib firm must have begun after that date.[15]

To become a citizen, Johann had to appear before the EWZ to determine his status in the Nazi state. My father's memory of his appearance before the commission centred on the group's realization that one of them was in fact Jewish. On the evening before their scheduled appearance, a Moscow student named Mettner confided to the group that he was Jewish and had been circumcised. After considerable discussion, the group decided to try to smuggle Mettner through the examination, which involved appearing entirely naked before a panel of seven doctors. Although it was touted as a medical exam, this appearance was actually one of the most important in the naturalization process because its primary aim was to examine the candidate's racial suitability. The ruse must have involved creating a suitable biography for Mettner and was helped by the fact that one member of the group, Schmidt, resembled him. It was decided that Schmidt would go through with Mettner's papers first and then, because they believed he would return to the group, come back after the examination and, after a number of the others had gone, go through again with his own papers. My father admitted that if it had not worked they all would have ended up in a concentration camp. But it did work; Mettner became a German citizen, like all the others. Through his contact with Mrs. Fast, Johann learned that Mettner later became an officer in the German Army.

The documents of the process of becoming a German citizen that have survived offer some additional insights into where my father stood regarding his previous life in the Soviet Union. On the citizenship commission forms, he noted that he had four sisters and a mother who were in the Soviet Union, but he declared himself to be single. There is no mention of a wife. There is also no mention of his being Mennonite; he indicated his own and his parents' religious affiliation as Lutheran. Although he likely began to use the German version of his name before becoming a German citizen, it is not clear exactly how and at what pace he switched from being Ivan to being Johann. All of his documents from this time give his name as Johann, even though in his earlier life he had been Hans and Ivan.

The Nazi system of assessing the suitability of ethnic Germans for membership in the *herrenvolk* ("master race") rendered Johann an ideal candidate for establishing German dominance in the east. One of the classification systems placed them in a *volksliste,* a category based on their racial suitability. Johann was classed as *volksliste ii* on a document that noted the relative length and width of his nose, the colour of his eyes and hair, and the shape of his head and cheekbones. Ethnic Germans in *volksliste i* and *ii* were eligible to be considered as settlers of the east. Hitler's dream was to populate the territory gained in Eastern Europe and the Soviet Union with racially and culturally suitable "true" Germans. In a second classification system, applicants could be classed as "O," "A," or "S." Category "O" settlers were to become the vanguard of Nazi domination of territories in Eastern Europe that would provide *lebensraum* for Germans. To qualify, one had to show evidence of cultural suitability. EWZ records dutifully record that Johann attended a German-language village school, that both his parents were German, and that he was fluent in German. As a result, he was placed in Category "O." Category "A" settlers were to be sent to the Reich proper to be culturally reintegrated, while Category "S" settlers were deemed unsuitable and sent out of the Warthegau. Documents note that Johann expressed a desire to be resettled in Ukraine.[16]

The period between my father's being drafted into the Red Army and his becoming a German citizen captures the range of how we marshal memories to create stories. The dramatic stories of first combat, coming under attack, and being captured were some of my father's most vivid stories—you could almost smell the dust and powder of explosions and taste the stagnant water. The surviving documents of his becoming German, and a German citizen, illustrate how my father had to become increasingly selective in the weaving of available memories into stories to maintain coherence with the image of himself he wanted to convey.

The stories of points of contact with the Jewish question offer an interesting window onto the transformation of his identity, the context of his storytelling, and the autobiographical image he was trying to project. Within days of his capture by the German military, Johann seems to have come into contact with the reality that Jews were being killed. He "knew" that politruks were Jewish and that they were being summarily shot. Although it is less clear what he and his friends knew about the consequences of Mettner's being discovered to be Jewish, it is apparent that they feared the worst. They also came face to face with the reality of their own safety if they fraternized with Jews and Poles, who were considered in Nazi ideology to be less than human or, in the case of Jews, devilishly superhuman.

It appears, however, that my father also chose his stories carefully. He told stories that painted himself in a positive light. In every case, he was either assisting Jews to prevent their sure execution or portraying himself as being dismayed or surprised at Nazi racial ideology. Given that the stories were told in a Canadian context in which the Holocaust is a potent memory and the complicity of ordinary Germans in its atrocities is controversial, the stories assembled autobiographical memories in ways that were acceptable to Canadian listeners.

Even in the absence of any direct conversation on becoming German, my father's stories conveyed the rapid transformation of his identity. Within days of being captured in the POW camps, Johann started to be German. Although there were some bumps in the road, such as the incident with the girls in Lublin and the harsh admonishment from the camp commander in Litzmannstadt, Johann did not seem to have any difficulty making the transition. Even then, my father's stories were sensitive to the social context of Canada and the reality of the Holocaust. My father chose to highlight his contact with the Jewish question in terms of how he had helped to save some Jews from sure death. His stories illustrated the creative reconstruction that we are capable of without violating the veracity of our stories.

The Fog of War

As part of his repertoire of war stories, my father narrated a series of anecdotes that seemed to fit between his becoming a German citizen and his participation in an artillery unit in the later part of the war. In his memory, becoming a part of the Wehrmacht followed closely on the heels of the process of acquiring German citizenship. The way he remembered it, almost immediately after becoming a German citizen, he received his *stellungsbefehl* or "draft order." In the same week that he was called up, the other nine in his group of friends also received their draft orders. Carl Leib, his employer in Pabianitz who was a lieutenant-colonel in the Luftwaffe, immediately offered to apply to keep Johann in his employ rather than in the military, but that was not possible. He then suggested that Johann report to his flying squadron in Prague, where he could train as a pilot and then fly under Leib's command. By then, though, Johann had lost his desire for air combat. He declined, claiming it was enough to be shot at on the ground. In an airplane, if you survived being shot at, you could still be killed when you crashed. His draft order required him to report to a large base near Prague known as the Hindenburg Kaserne, where he once again began basic training. It had lasted only a few days when he was asked to step forward during a marching drill because his style of turning did not match what was being taught. The officer in charge asked him where he had learned to turn like that—probably in rather unpleasant tones. Johann replied, "Pardon me, but I have served before in another army." The officer immediately wanted to know which army; when Johann indicated it had been the Red Army, he was immediately asked to "fall in." Later that day he had to report to the officers' quarters, where he faced more questions about his strange military history. By then, they knew more about him, including the fact that he was a trained mechanic and tank driver. Johann was not required to participate in marching drills after that. When the call came for those with inside duties to "fall out," he went to the repair shop, where he spent the day repairing army vehicles. Over time, they promised Johann he would never be sent to the eastern front and changed his documents to indicate he had been born a German in Angerapp, East Prussia.[1]

Later Johann became a driving instructor, a job similar to one he had had in the Red Army. His task was to train recruits how to drive a truck. Each day he took new drivers through the city in a medium-sized truck, like the one he had driven for Carl Leib, to a large training area where he taught them driving skills. When they knew the basics, he allowed them to drive in the city. Each morning he took a new pair of recruits, allowing one to drive to the training area and the other to drive back. The pattern was repeated each afternoon. Before he was ready for combat, he had to be trained to drive a half-track, known as a *Zugmaschine,* which pulled large cannons for an artillery brigade. This was not a difficult task, my father recalled, because he had driven a variety of combat vehicles and trucks by then. All of these activities, according to his stories, took place as part of his first and only unit, an artillery unit that he always referred to as the Heeres Artillerie Brigade 401.

A dramatic story, which my father placed immediately after he completed his training in Prague, began with Johann and forty others being assembled to join the Afrika Korps, the popular designation for German forces fighting in North Africa under Field Marshal Erwin Rommel. In a formal interview with my father, he placed this event in spring, probably April. It seemed that a group of technical personnel, such as electricians, mechanics, and communications specialists, were being assembled to be sent to Africa to assist Rommel's forces there. Johann had not volunteered for the reassignment but had been selected.[2]

When asked if he wanted to join the mission to Africa, Johann declined, claiming to be unfamiliar with Africa and pointing out he had grown up in a cold climate and did not believe he was suited for the job. In his account, my father noted that, while one could express an opinion in such circumstances, it did not mean that anything changed, and while they chuckled at his reference to having cold climate origins he ended up being "volunteered" anyway. About forty people like him were assembled in Prague and given a few hours of instruction on using a parachute, and they made a few practice jumps. After this brief training, they were assembled and sent by train to Italy. Along with other such groups, they detrained at a large air base somewhere south of Rome. My father only vaguely remembered that they arrived at a place with a lot of soldiers' barracks and a nearby village whose name he could not recall. They spent a day in Italy preparing for their mission. They received new beige uniforms with Afrika Korps and other insignias on them. Early in the morning, they were loaded onto airplanes. In my father's recollection, some sixty airplanes took off for Africa. The twin-engine aircraft had no seats, so the forty or so in his group sat on parachutes and backpacks between the ribs of the fuselage.

My father thought they had been airborne approximately half an hour when they came under fire from the British Navy. Although they were flying at a high altitude, anti-aircraft fire brought down a few of the planes. In their case, the left-side engine was hit and caught fire. The propeller made a few more revolutions and then stopped. Soon a long flame was streaming from the engine, and the pilot banked the plane to keep the flames from engulfing it. By then, all of the soldiers were being ordered to bail out because the airplane was too heavily loaded for one engine. It had a large door, and they were ordered to jump in groups of seven. The parachutes they had been issued automatically deployed when they reached a predetermined altitude. They were instructed to set the dial at a certain altitude, press the button that activated the release mechanism, and jump. Johann was one of the first to the door, and by the time he jumped out the interior of the aircraft was already filling with smoke, to the extent that it was almost suffocating. After jumping out, he remembered looking up and seeing burning pieces of the disintegrating aircraft falling to the sea below. By the time his parachute opened, he could no longer see the airplane and did not know what eventually happened to it.

Although he did not think he had lost consciousness entirely, my father recalled being surprised at one point in the descent when he realized they were above water. The seven in his group all landed successfully near each other. One of them was the radio operator, who was unconscious when he landed; the others had to get to him quickly before he drowned. They cut the lines on their parachutes and used them to lash themselves together so they would not drift apart. After some time, they managed to use the radio to make contact with a German submarine. Then they waited. Eight hours later the submarine appeared, having surfaced nearby without them being aware of it. They were quickly taken aboard before the submarine submerged again. They had to be helped aboard because they found it difficult to walk after hanging for eight hours in salt water. When they were safely inside and the submarine was below the surface again, there was a lot of discussion among the submarine's crew about firing torpedoes at an Allied ship, but that idea was abandoned, and they made for Italy.

An ambulance was waiting for them when they arrived, and they were taken to a hospital, where they spent a few days. It was not clear from my father's recollections whether they arrived in Venice or were taken there later, but after being released from hospital Johann ended up being part of the Venice harbour patrol. As my father recalled, the next few weeks were some of the best of his army days. He was part of a patrol boat crew that watched over the ocean near the entrance to the Venice harbour to prevent sea mines from floating into the city. A sea mine was a large metal sphere with spoke-like protrusions. It was filled with explosives, and each spoke had a glass end, which broke when it hit something and detonated the mine. The job for the crew of the boat on which Johann worked was to spot the mines, sound an alarm to warn people in the city to open their windows, and then use a machine gun to fire at the glass ends of the spokes to detonate the mine. My father recalled one occasion when they caught sight of a mine quite late when it was close to the city and had to detonate it almost immediately after sounding the alarm, hoping that the windows in Venice would not all shatter from the force of the explosion. If there were no mines to explode, the crew basked in the sun. According to his recollection, my father patrolled the Venice harbour for a number of weeks before returning to Czechoslovakia. During his time away, his unit had moved from Prague to Pilsen (Plzeň).

The greatest threat to his life during the entire war came when Johann was wounded by partisans in the forests east of Warsaw. My father usually began this story by noting that there had been a call to donate clothing for transport to the eastern front, where the troops were in desperate need of winter clothing. In winter, probably January, Johann joined a convoy of eighty trucks after loading "furs, felt boots, whatever you could imagine."[3] The convoy drivers were warned that there were partisans along their route and that they should be careful, particularly after their last refuelling stop east of Warsaw. The convoy was accompanied by the NSKK (National Socialist Motoring Corps), a Nazi party organization involved in transport, together with a number of Panzerspeewagon, light armoured vehicles. True to the warning, the convoy was attacked by partisans and came under heavy fire in the forests east of Warsaw. My father recalled noticing the windshield break, and then felt warmness in his chest. He managed to stop the truck before he lost consciousness. A bullet from a partisan who had fired at them from the forested edge of the road had entered the rear of the truck cab, passing through his chest before exiting through the windshield. It had passed within inches of his heart, and while it had shattered some of his ribs miraculously no major organ had been hit.

My father had no memories of what happened after that, but apparently he was taken to a first-aid station a few miles up the road, where he was stabilized. He was evacuated by a Fiseler Storch, a small airplane that made a number of cameo appearances in his stories. It was usually used as a reconnaissance aircraft, but some versions were also used as air ambulances. Johann awoke from his unconscious state in a hospital in Prague. It took time for the wound to heal since bone fragments from the shattered ribs kept on causing abscesses, and surgeries were required to remove them. Johann spent a number of weeks in the hospital, where he broke the rules by sitting up when he was supposed to be lying down. My father was apparently quite a hit with the nurses, and occasionally he told stories of how he flirted and went to the movies with them. On one occasion, his wound began to bleed while at a movie, but he put pressure on it to stop the bleeding until they got back. The story had different endings. In one telling, he simply returned to Litzmannstadt after recovering in the Prague hospital. In a more common version, he was in the hospital in Prague for a few months and then went to Bavaria for convalescence.

The Bavarian connection came by way of a doctor in the Prague hospital who had family there. When the doctor realized Johann had no family to go home to for his convalescent leave, he suggested that Johann might enjoy visiting his brother on the family farm in Bavaria. Johann took the train to a village, Osseck am Wald, near the city of Hof in Bavaria, not far from the Czechoslovak border, where he spent a few weeks on a farm. He did farm work, mostly mowing hay, but was only required to work as much as his health allowed. The food was delicious, and with main meals and breaks they ate six times a day. My father received no salary, but the farmer gave him a little spending money.[4] It was never clear from his stories who owned the farm. A widow whose husband had been killed in the war was there, as was an older man, either her father or the father of her husband. It seems the widow was attracted to Johann, and in a rarely told anecdote my father related how one day she had sat on her bed wrapped in paper with a large bow and presented herself to him as a gift. He had apparently graciously declined.

The account of the end of his leave involved travel back to his unit by train. Johann was tired and had fallen asleep in his seat when an officer who had boarded at one of the stops came into the car. The officer severely reprimanded him for not promptly offering the Nazi salute. My father excused himself and in his later account of this event explained that, while he had been on leave, the attempted assassination of Hitler had taken place. As part of the retribution for the attempt on his life by members of the Wehrmacht, Hitler had ruled that Wehrmacht soldiers were also required to give the Nazi salute.

My father also told somewhat unconnected stories of being near Paris as part of a transport unit. In one version, immediately after returning from patrolling the Venice harbour, he was part of a unit sent to France. The unit was not sent all the way to the Normandy coast, but somewhere west of Paris, approximately twenty kilometres from the point on the coast where the Allies landed on D-Day. He did not think the landings had taken place when he arrived; in his recollection, they occurred shortly thereafter. One story fragment seemed to corroborate that they arrived there before D-Day. Johann was occasionally called upon to serve as chauffeur for officers. On one such trip, he drove officers to the coast, simply because they wanted to see the ocean.

My father remembered the retreat through Paris more than a month after D-Day more clearly. Parisians were already anticipating the liberation, and there were uprisings in the city. German tanks fired on the French resistance, and Johann and every other motorized vehicle "had to take everything in Paris," "everything that was German," with them. They loaded their vehicles with nurses, communications assistants, known as *blitzmädchen,* and other support personnel. When they had retreated some forty or fifty kilometres east of Paris, the various personnel they had collected were gradually reassigned.[5]

Another story from the area around Paris involved flying. Johann was frequently assigned the task of getting parts to complete the repair jobs he undertook as a mechanic and driver. On one occasion, he was to use any available flight, and he joined a flight to Munich. A highlight for him was the opportunity to fly the airplane. My father claimed that for about an hour the pilot caught a few winks of sleep while he flew the plane.[6]

As these vignettes demonstrate, most of my father's war stories were told without reference to specific dates. As an ordinary soldier, my father was usually unconscious of the overall progress of the war or even the battles of which he was a part. His stories often began with reference to a month or season—spring, April, fall—but were otherwise seldom anchored chronologically. Occasionally he tied together vignettes, noting that a second story occurred after an earlier one. I heard these stories from when I was a boy and knew very little of the history of the Second World War. As I became more interested in history and began to interview my father formally, I probed his accounts more directly to try to fit his personal stories into the broader story of the war. Between the more formal taped interviews, I also searched for documentary sources that would corroborate his accounts or at least place them in historical context.

The transcript of his military record from the Deutsche Dienstelle provides a way of grounding his stories of being drafted more firmly in time. According to these records, my father was drafted in October 1943, a full year after he first appeared before the naturalization commissions in the Warthegau. The first unit to which he was assigned was not the 401 but one denoted the Stm. Battr. le. Art. Ers. U. Ausb. Abt. (m) 103,[7] a motorized light artillery replacement and training unit. It would take another eleven months, until September 1944, before the 401 of his memory would be formed.

The story of the Mediterranean adventure offers the clearest example of the problem of locating my father's memories in time. His story of this event never wavered from situating it in time after he was drafted. However, Germany's hold on the African continent was eliminated when the German Army surrendered in Tunis on 12 May 1943. In the weeks before the surrender, Germany mounted a large airlift to supply the troops. In April 1943, a large number of these transport airplanes were shot down, most of them by fighter aircraft rather than by the British Navy.[8] That suggests that the story of parachuting into the Mediterranean likely took place in April 1943, when Johann had not yet been drafted into the German Army. Clearly the Mediterranean adventure was not part of his experiences as a soldier but occurred the spring before he was drafted. Perhaps my father confused being drafted into the Wehrmacht with a call-up for service in one of Nazi Germany's quasi-military organizations, such as the Organization Todt (OT) and the Reichsarbeitsdienst (RAD), which provided engineering and labour for the German military effort.

Johann's neglect in saluting properly on the train because he was unaware of the order requiring the Wehrmacht to use the Nazi salute places the story shortly after the attempted assassination of Hitler in the summer of 1944. A group of conspirators had plotted to assassinate him by placing a briefcase with a bomb in the room where he was to meet his generals to plan and conduct the war. The bomb exploded, but another officer had moved the briefcase in the interim, and the heavy legs of the table apparently deflected the blast, sparing Hitler. Since the plot had been the work of Wehrmacht officers, Hitler responded a few days later, on 24 July, with an order that all Wehrmacht soldiers were to use the Nazi salute, previously reserved for the SS and party organizations. Since the attempted assassination took place in July 1944, Johann's trip east of Warsaw and subsequent wound from a sniper's bullet must have taken place in the winter of 1943–44.[9]

The excerpt of his military service record offers little help in sorting out the temporal context of the vignettes in France. His military record notes that, as of 30 October 1943, Johann was assigned to his first unit, the 103, a motorized light artillery replacement and training unit. On 15 April 1944, the unit designation changed to the Marschbattr. Art. Ers. u. Ausb. Abt. 103, which in German military organization noted a change to non-active status, likely due to his being wounded. The change might have coincided with his conva- lescence in Prague and Bavaria.[10] There is no recorded change to indicate that his transport experiences around Paris took place while Johann was assigned to the 103, but it is possible that, after returning from Bavaria in July 1944, he returned to his unit near Paris in time to be part of the retreat through the city in August. By September, however, he was back in Czechoslovakia, where the Heeres Artillerie Brigade 401, the unit that my father remembered most clearly, was being assembled. The timeline for being shot while he was travelling east of Warsaw would then shift back to January 1944, a few months after he became part of the replacement and training unit, the 103.

Memory is not infallible, and as Ulrich Neisser suggests it is "not like playing back a tape or looking at a picture." He concludes that "some memory stories do achieve a kind of stability—especially if they have been frequently repeated—but their accuracy cannot be presumed simply because they are vivid and clear."[11] My probing of my father's stories with the aim of placing them accurately in a chronological sequence in the greater narrative of the

Second World War disrupted the script that my father had maintained for years. Attempts to rescript his memory tended only to raise other problems of chronological sequencing. Anchoring one story in the Second World War timeline based on some recognizable aspect invariably forced other stories he told out of sequence. Clearly he joined threads of stories together in ways that while true, in the sense that he experienced them, did not fit together with the events of the war of which they were a part.

My father's stories were also never challenged or mediated by others who had the same or similar experiences. Memories and the stories that arise from them are often collaborative projects, undertaken in the presence of others who experienced the same events, though from different perspectives. Siblings in a family, a husband and wife, or comrades offer the best examples. My father told these stories for more than forty years, and in all that time there was no one to challenge his memories. He was completely separated from anyone who shared these experiences and with whom he might have been forced to collaborate in creating his narrative.

It is also apparent that the period between the summer of 1942 and the fall of 1944 was comprised of intense activity for Johann and that he partici-pated in dramatic and life-threatening events. Although speculative to some extent, a reconstruction of the time period illustrates the frenetic pace of his life during these years. In June 1942, he got his driver's licence and sometime after that began working for Carl Leib; in November 1942, he became a German citizen. He might have made a trip to the east with clothes for the troops with Carl Leib's truck in January 1943 and then went on the abortive trip to Africa in April of that year. Johann then spent a few weeks in Venice during the early summer of 1943 before returning to Czechoslovakia to be drafted into the German Army. As a member of his first unit, he likely made a trip to Paris in the fall of 1943 and then was sent to the eastern front with supplies in January 1944, where he was wounded. He spent the late winter of 1944 in the hospital in Prague before going to the farm in Bavaria in April. In July 1944, Johann was heading back to his unit only to be dispatched to the western front, where he took part in the retreat through Paris in August. By September, he was back in Pilsen for the formation of the Heeres Artillerie Brigade 401.

The stories of experiences after his capture by the Germans represented a careful negotiation between what my father remembered and the desire to guard the image of the person he wanted to portray to his listeners. Given these constraints, it is not surprising that his memory linked events that oc-curred at different times, that he confused locations of events, and that he conflated time. As Geoffrey Cubitt puts it, "remembering seems indissolubly coupled with forgetting... a quest for points of recognition across territory of the more or less forgotten whose features we never succeed in bringing into stable focus."[12]

There was also the opportunity to create artifacts of memory from other sources. My father mentioned seeing the Wochenschau, a weekly propaganda newsreel shown in theatres before the feature film of the night. The newsreels "reported" on the events of the war and offered dramatic visual footage and commentary. It is likely that what he saw and heard interfered with, and in some cases supplanted, memories of his experiences.

Finally the pursuit of documentary evidence to corroborate his stories brought to light information on his personal relationships that also shed light on how my father told his stories of this period. He seems not to have been able to incorporate all that he experienced into the autobiographical person he wanted to project. His military record extract indicates that his home address was: Ehefrau (wife) Frieda Werner, Babianitz Krs. Lask, Wiesengasse 6. Based on this fragment of information, my father must have remarried sometime in 1942 or 1943 while he was in the Warthegau. He never mentioned being mar-ried a second time during his time in German-occupied Poland. The only other reference to a relationship with a woman named Frieda came in difficult con-versations with my mother much later. During the weeks after my father's death in 2003, my mother in her grief mentioned that, when she first met Johann after the war, he carried a photo of an attractive woman named Frieda. At the time, Johann had been interested in my mother's half-sister, Tina. When my mother and father began courting, the photo disappeared, and they never discussed Frieda again. The autobiographical person my father wanted to create for his listeners did not allow for that story to be told and must have interfered with his stories of the experiences of that period.

The 401

THE AIM OF LOCATING MY FATHER'S STORY within the bigger story of the events of the Second World War was easier to achieve for the period between when Johann became part of the Heeres Artillerie Brigade (mot.) 401 in September 1944 and his capture by Allied forces in April 1945. The 401 was the only unit my father had clear memories of belonging to. In fact, listening to his stories of being a German soldier, it seemed he was part of the 401 for all that time.

His memories of the period when he was active on the front were never specific with reference to the larger story of the war. Only a general sense of the battles, times, and places in which my father participated could be gained from them. He did, however, have a story about the process of the 401 being assembled and then becoming an active unit. As he explained it, when a soldier was sent somewhere, he had to report to the army reporting centre in that area. In the formal interviews, he conveyed the sense of losing the power to decide where one was going. As he put it, "they just told you when the train left for a certain place, gave you a card, and you packed your backpack, and away you went."[1] In his case, he arrived at Strassitz and then was sent to Pilsen, where the 401 was being assembled. The unit needed Zugmaschine drivers, and he was one of them.

After being transferred to Pilsen, Johann's battalion was outfitted with new equipment, and they began a month of training together as a unit. Here Johann also met a fellow soldier, Zachada, with whom he participated in many adventures and occasionally trouble. When I pressed my father for this friend's identity, he could only recall that he was from Czechoslovakia, that his family was somehow connected to the name of the large arms manufacturer Škoda, that they always called him Zachada, and that his last name could have been Miller or something like that.

Sometime in the fall, the newly assembled unit became active. They all assembled at the train station, where their equipment was loaded, and off they went. Ordinary soldiers were usually not told exactly where they were headed and did not travel in great comfort. It was already cold, and Johann and the others sat in their machines and kept warm by using Esbit heaters. They were headed toward France, and the train travelled only at night and was occasionally delayed for a few hours while the track was repaired.[2]

I recall my father telling a story about the process of loading the trains that had more detail than the above anecdote taken from the formal interviews. Entraining the inexperienced unit was a mass of confusion, and many of the Zugmaschine drivers were not up to driving their large machines up the narrow ramps onto the train cars. An officer was yelling and swearing at the delays, so Johann offered to drive all the remaining machines onto the rail cars. He jumped into one machine after another, and soon the entire battery's Zugmaschines were loaded. The officer promoted him on the spot to the rank of *gefreiter* ("lance corporal") and assured him he would soon get his new shoulder patches. The promotion never happened, and he remained an ordinary soldier for the remainder of the war.

Along with stories of specific events, my father frequently offered explanations of various details of equipment and military procedures. As he explained, an artillery unit was seldom right on the front lines of a battle. In the German army system, half-tracks, such as the Zugmaschine driven by Johann, pulled cannons into specified firing positions some distance from the battle line. A battery's group of six cannons had a maximum range of fifteen to twenty kilometres, which meant the firing position was within that distance of the target.[3] From the battery's firing position, a cable was rolled out on the ground toward the main battle line by a tracked motorcycle. The cable provided communication between the forward observer and the firing officer. The forward observer provided target data and checked that the shells were on target. In the early part of their time on the western front, the unit made use of a reconnaissance aircraft, a Fiseler Storch, which served in the role of forward observer. My father's fascination with airplanes meant the Storch made frequent appearances in his stories. In one anecdote that reinforced his fascination with airplanes, my father recalled with fondness servicing the plane and making friends with the pilot. The pilot occasionally took Johann along on a reconnaissance flight, but eventually the flights were stopped because of Allied domination of the skies, and a ground observer became the only method of artillery observation.[4]

After the Zugmaschine had pulled the cannon into place, it left the firing position to park in what was called the trossraum. This rear area was some distance behind the firing position and was where equipment was maintained and supplies and ammunition were assembled to support the unit in battle. Johann spent most of his time in this rear area. As my father explained, even though he was the driver of a machine that pulled cannons, he was also a mechanic and could be stationed at one place for two weeks or more. In these rear areas, his machine, which had a mounted anti-aircraft gun, was parked somewhere to protect a potential target, such as an airport. The cannons were large, and all he could remember was that their calibre was "twelve something." He seemed to recall they could fire a shell at targets up to forty kilometres away with the "eighth charge."[5]

Johann worked as a mechanic in a large tent, and when the battle line began to encroach on the firing positions, or when they were discovered and targeted by the opposing artillery or aircraft, the Zugmaschine drivers had to make their way to the firing positions to get the cannons and transport them to new firing positions. This was the most dangerous time for a Zugmaschine driver since shifting firing positions often occurred under enemy fire or when the enemy was nearby.

One of my father's stories involved the process of laying the cable for the ground observer. A soldier named Schneider drove the tracked motorcycle that rolled out the wire toward the battle line. An officer from his battery ordered Johann to have a look at the motorcycle because Schneider was not making it to the battle line with the cable—the motorcycle was always breaking down. Johann looked it over and, aside from making some minor adjustments, determined there was nothing wrong with it. The officer then suggested that Johann accompany Schneider to the firing positions to make sure he got there. They drove the motorcycle to where the cannons were set up without incident, but upon arriving there they were advised to immediately dig foxholes because the positions might come under fire at any time. They each dug a foxhole near to, but not right next to, each other. They had just finished when enemy artillery shells began to land on their location. When it was over, Johann emerged from his foxhole to find that nothing was left of Schneider or his foxhole. There were just shreds of clothing and body parts hanging from nearby trees. A shell had scored a direct hit on his foxhole. My father believed that Schneider had had a premonition that his "number was up" and intentionally rigged his motorcycle so he would not make it to the front. Johann was able to recover Schneider's watch, and he inquired about and noted his home address. He kept the watch until the end of the war, and after his release he looked up the Schneider family. They lived in a large house in Wurzburg, and Schneider had been their only son. The older couple invited Johann into their home, served him tea, and had a brief conversation about their son and how he had died.

The story of Schneider's death illustrated a common characteristic of my father's war stories. It was told without emotion, matter-of-factly. One could not discern from the way my father told this horrible story whether Schneider had been a friend or barely an acquaintance. The event seemed to leave a mark on his emotions, since he took the trouble to visit Schneider's parents long after it. Layers of repetitive storytelling seem to have insulated him from the emotions he experienced at the time and some time thereafter. The story of Schneider's death was also somewhat unusual in that it was told in the context of seeing many other acquaintances die, both before and after Schneider. It seems that the arbitrary nature of his death—both had been in the same situation, in foxholes beside each other, with each having an equal chance of being killed—made the event memorable. My father survived, and Schneider did not.

Although my father never distinguished times of rest and refit from his other stories, there were clearly times when his unit was not directly engaged in combat. It was probably during such a time that Zachada and Johann decided, given the meagre soldier's rations and notoriously bad cooking, to find their own stock of food. They raided the smokehouses of local farmers and arrived back in camp with arms loaded with sausages. Needless to say, they were severely reprimanded for their adventure.

"When we were in the Schnee Eiffel for the big attack" signalled a story of my father's participation in what I would later come to understand was what Americans referred to as the Battle of the Bulge in the Ardennes Forest of Belgium and Luxembourg. In his memory, they drove two nights and two days to get to Belgium. My father recalled the road being called "Napolean's

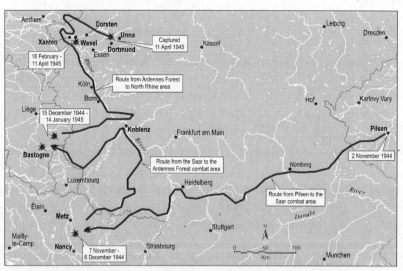

Map 5. Movements of the 401 Artillery Brigade, 1943–45.

Strasse," and they drove only during the night; during the day, they hid the machines. He remembered getting to their positions at 10:00 p.m., only two hours before the midnight deadline, and "at twelve o'clock the thunder began."[6]

In other accounts, my father remembered more graphically the scream of the German rocket launchers known as *nebelwerfer* and vividly recalled the impressive thunder of the artillery. The rocket launchers with their eight rocket-loaded tubes made a terrible noise when they were launched.[7] The opening days of the battle were successful for the German Army, and they advanced for ten days before beginning to falter. On Christmas day, Johann, along with two others and the unit's doctor, took the Zugmaschine to get supplies from abandoned American depots not far from where they were. They came across a large warehouse filled with "chocolates, chocolate bars, these big boxes of food stuffs, rows of tanks were parked there, not one of them had moved." Johann and those with him loaded the entire machine with K-rations; "that was our Christmas present. Hitler had said that if we wanted a Christmas present we could go and get it from the Americans." The battle went well for a few days after that, but then the Germans ran out of fuel, and the advance had not made it as far as the fuel dumps.[8]

Likely it was on one of these days, while they had camouflaged their units in the forest, that the Zugmaschine drivers watched as American airplanes strafed a truck convoy along the road in front of the forest where they were encamped. A German anti-aircraft gun nearby fired at an Allied fighter–bomber, which immediately crashed near them. The plane came down so hard that the engine separated and rolled some distance away from the rest of the wreckage. Nothing had happened to the pilot, who got out immediately and seemed intent on destroying what was left of the plane with some kind of pistol. Johann and his fellow drivers yelled at the surprised pilot, who had thought he was alone, and made him sit down on a nearby tree stump until he could be taken away. They spoke German to him, and Johann noticed that, while he spoke poorly, he answered in recognizable Mennonite Low German, and he learned that he had a Mennonite name and was from Canada. Johann visited with him, explaining he would be a prisoner of war and assuring him he would be treated well. He "told him there he would be wearing a tie, pressed pants," and the food would all come from Switzerland. The pilot asked Johann to retrieve a package from the airplane that had "cigarettes, soap, chocolate, a few chocolate bars, and other things to eat," which he then distributed. After some time, two officers, one of whom spoke English, arrived in a jeep and took the pilot away.[9]

There were dangerous moments in the Ardennes battles. According to one version of my father's stories, his unit received a new commander whose inexperience resulted in their battery remaining in its firing positions too long. The American artillery had fired a targeting round at them during the day, and then at night the firing positions of the battery came under heavy shelling. Four of the six cannons survived. Johann loaded his half-track with a number of wounded soldiers who had been concealed behind a haystack. He was finally able to make it to a medical station, but by the time he got there most of them had died. He took the bodies to a bombed-out schoolhouse, where another hundred soldiers had died. After unloading the bodies, Johann drove his machine into a small river, where he used a shovel and river water to wash off the blood and gore. In my father's memory, some thirty soldiers from his battery were killed that day.

In another story possibly about the same event, my father noted that they had been unable to reposition their cannons, and "during the night the Americans broke through with their tanks." They had to leave in a hurry at night, driving through the same village where "a short distance ahead there was an American tank."[10]

Johann was frequently called upon to take equipment to rear areas and sometimes well into Germany for repair or to bring up new equipment from factories. On one such occasion, likely when the brigade had withdrawn from the Ardennes combat area, he made a day's journey to pull a cannon back for repairs. Along the road, he came upon dead German soldiers hanging from trees. SS soldiers stopped him, and he had to show them his orders. After he passed inspection, he asked what the soldiers had done to earn being executed. The reply was that they were deserters and "didn't want to fight anymore, they wanted to go home." My father found out later that they had actually been wounded and noted that such actions resulted in hatred between SS and Wehrmacht soldiers. The SS "were very strict, soldiers were not supposed to go home, they were all supposed to fight."[11]

After the 401 left the Ardennes forest, the Allies advanced rapidly, and soon the German Army had its back to the Rhine River. In the face of renewed Allied attacks, the Rhine became a major barrier for the 401 to cross. They arrived at the riverbank at night in a forested area where they had to wait for a ferry that could take only four machines at a time. They were in a lineup most of the night but finally crossed the Rhine and drove a short distance before stopping. There seemed to be a lot of confusion about where they were supposed to be, and it took a few days for things to settle down.[12]

As with many of his memories of the war, my father's stories were so disconnected that it was difficult to determine at what point in the war each took place. One notable example was the struggle to place the stories about a break from combat in Holland. The unit arrived in Holland at night, and after Johann dropped off his cannon at its firing position he drove his machine into a barn and went to sleep. He awoke to the soothing sounds of milk streaming into a pail. He realized he was parked between the rows of cows, and it was milking time for the Dutch farmer. He switched on his radio and, knowing the Dutch were not enthusiastic about their German occupiers, tuned it to a British station that broadcast propaganda even though they were expressly forbidden to listen to foreign stations. The sounds of the milk streaming into the pail became slower and more irregular as the farmer began to listen to the broadcast. When Johann got out of the Zugmaschine to introduce himself, he soon made a friend, who was curious about whether he was allowed to listen to such broadcasts. When Johann assured him it was entirely forbidden and begged him not to tell anyone, the farmer's goodwill was assured. It turned out the farmer had a number of attractive daughters and tried to convince Johann to abandon the war, which he thought was almost over anyway, and stay to live with them. They found out that Johann's Mennonite Low German and the farmer's Dutch were similar enough that they could understand each other remarkably well. Johann's memory of the soldiers hanging from trees in the Ardennes likely made desertion a remote possibility, but it helped to make the stay in Holland a fond memory.

In a number of interviews interspersed with my research on the events on the western front, my father and I tried to fix the dates of the Holland stories. Although he could place them after the battles in the Ardennes, his only time frame for remembering when he had been in Holland was a memory of the apple blossoms being on the trees. That memory placed the events in spring. In one exchange, I asked the question a number of times:

But can you remember when that would have been?

No, it was in spring, that I know. First we came to Germany, right across the border, we were there for a while, and then, then we came to Holland. No, first we came to Holland, and when we came to Germany we were in the Ruhr area, that was our end....

But you cannot remember when that was?

It was early in spring; it could have been in the beginning of May.

It must have been much earlier, you see this is 1945, 1944–45, and you see in April you were already captured. This must have been earlier.

I always judge the time by the weather, the weather was pleasant, and the fruit trees were blooming, but of course they bloom earlier there, they probably bloom in April already.[13]

The above series of stories was typical of my father's stories of his time in the German Army. In broad terms, it was clear that they occurred after the Allies had landed and retaken most of France. References to the Battle of the Bulge and the crossing of the Rhine River fixed some of the stories in time. However, it was difficult to get a sense of what part his unit played in the various battles. Between formal taped interviews with my father in the 1980s, I was pursuing research on the military history of the war on the western front and trying to locate additional sources in German military archives. Although details of the 401's role in the war were mentioned only in passing in the military histories of the western front, a sense of the kind of unit the 401 was gradually emerged. It was an artillery brigade of five battalions, with each battalion consisting of two batteries. A battery was made up of a number of cannons, usually six. In December 1944, the unit had seventy-two guns of wide assortment, ranging in size from the 75 mm field cannon to the 152 mm captured Russian howitzer that was operated by one junior officer and eight soldiers and fired a 43.5 kg shell.[14]

Some good fortune also produced additional sources in the German military archives that shed light on the activities of the 401. In my initial contact with the archives, staff advised me that the unit was small, and due to space limitations war diaries for units below the division level were generally not available. Fortunately, however, they had received a small collection of records that included the war diaries of the 5th Battalion of the 401. Although Johann was likely in the 2nd Battalion, this find provided daily records of the 401 through the lens of an official war diary recorded at or near the times of the events it described. Daily diaries were kept by an officer of the unit and varied somewhat in content, depending on the diarist. They recorded military details such as where the unit was stationed, when it went into battle, significant events of its engagements, and notations about enemy activity. The 401's diary collection also included the written orders kept on file by the 5th Battalion, some of which emanated from brigade headquarters, and they offered a window onto the more general events in which the 401 participated.[15]

The war diaries record the formation of the Heeres Artillerie Brigade (mot.) 401 on 30 September 1944. It was formed as a unit of Wehrkreis XIII, the military district that included portions of Bavaria and the area of Bohemia in Czechoslovakia. Its official training and replacement unit was the 103, the unit Johann had been assigned to after being drafted in October 1943.[16] On 2 November 1944, the Heeres Artillerie Brigade (mot.) 401 became an active unit.[17] That meant that the 401 was soon loaded onto trains for transport to the western front. My father's memories of loading the Zugmaschines coincided with these events. The unit arrived in the Saar region, just east of a line between the French cities of Nancy and Metz, on 7 November 1944.

Insertion of the 401 into the Saar battles must have been as much for testing and gaining combat experience as anything else since it was engaged in battle for only eight days. During that time, it was to assist the 11th Panzer Division in an attack. That attack either never materialized or was overtaken by General Patton's Third Army offensive, which began on 8 November. The

401 was unable to take up the position it had been ordered to occupy and then had to withdraw even farther almost immediately. In the emotionless summary of the first day of combat, the diarist noted that "in the evening the unit prepared to change position because of the situation and unsuitable firing opportunities.... The 13th battery already made its move in the evening because of losses." In the details that followed, the diarist curtly noted that at 18:00 the "firing position of the 13th battery was hit by enemy artillery fire, 1 dead, 3 seriously wounded, a number of lighter wounds," and nineteen minutes later he noted "further artillery fire on the firing position of the 13th battery, 1 wounded."[18] Even during the brief engagement, the unit was constantly short of ammunition, and sometimes firing orders had to be curtailed because of the dearth of ammunition. According to the war diary, the 401 was engaged in the Saar battles from 9 to 17 November, when it was withdrawn from the front to go into reserve. Two days before going into reserve, while engaged in heavy fighting, the unit was renamed the Volksartillerie Korps (mot.) 401, an apparent move by Hitler to recognize the participation of ethnic Germans such as Johann and to appeal to the unity of the German people. My father had no memory of the unit's change of name; he always referred to it by its earlier designation. During the two weeks the unit was in reserve, extensive orders came down for training and refitting it. The replacement of fifteen officers and sixteen regular soldiers in the 2nd Battalion alone might offer some hint of the losses experienced in the unit's first taste of combat.

The diarist noted that at 4:30 p.m. on 5 December 1944 at a meeting of the unit's commanders the corps was advised that orders to move from the Saar to another area would arrive within twenty-four hours. At 1:00 p.m. the next day, the 5th Battalion received orders that it would be entraining that evening. Due to Allied dominance of the skies and the absolute secrecy surrounding the buildup of troops, transports travelled only at night, when their movements did not invite the attention of *jabos,* as the diarist called Allied fighter–bombers. The corps travelled north from the Saar to the area east of the Ardennes forest by train. It arrived in Meisburg on 11 December, unloaded, and then moved forward under cover of darkness from 12 to 14 December. This creeping forward and driving only at night for a few days might be the memory my father had of driving to the Ardennes. Orders for the attack itself arrived at the 5th Battalion at 11:00 p.m. on 15 December.[19]

In my father's memory, the artillery shelling for the attack in the Ardennes forest began at midnight, but according to the war diaries the attack began at

5:30 a.m. My father also recalled that the crescendo of artillery fire culminated in the cannons of his unit joining the attack, but according to the war diaries the 401's guns remained silent in the early hours of the attack. General Hasso von Manteuffel had ordered there be no artillery preparation in the area in front of the 401 to allow the infantry to slip unnoticed through the widely spaced American positions in the wooded area of their sector.[20] It was not until 8:30 a.m. that the 5th Battalion's diarist recorded that the corps began firing at enemy targets, and by then the attack had moved beyond the Our River, which marked the initial line between the opposing forces. In the next few days, however, the corps was heavily involved in supporting the attack.[21]

My father's memory of venturing out with the Zugmaschine to collect booty from abandoned U.S. Army warehouses was also noted by the diarist of the 5th Battalion, who reported that on 19 December, "in the area around Ouren, the battalion captured a large quantity of booty in terms of vehicles, communications equipment, weapons, and rations."[22]

The town of Bastogne never came up in my father's stories. My father seemingly had no knowledge or memory of the drama that unfolded in the area around this relatively small place in Belgium. Bastogne had been surrounded by German troops during the initial thrust of the battle, but they had been unable to capture it in spite of repeated attempts. On 26 December, units of the U.S. Army broke through to relieve the beleaguered forces there. The relief of Bastogne signalled the beginning of the end for the German attack, but Hitler became even more determined to capture the town. On 29 December, the 401 was moved forward to support a renewed attack.

The dramatic stories of Johann having to transport large numbers of wounded and dying soldiers after the unit was shelled cannot be placed clearly in the diaries. The war diaries of the 5th Battalion do offer some hints, however, of where these events might have taken place. After firing on roads and intersections just outside Bastogne for the first few days, the corps was forced to move back toward the villages of Oberwampach and Niederwampach on 8 January 1945. The 5th Battalion's 13th and temporarily assigned 9th Batteries came under heavy shelling from the Americans during the next few days. It is likely that the events my father described took place in the same area.

In 1990, while on a trip to Germany to visit his sisters, who had just arrived there from the Soviet Union, I took my father on a trip through the areas where his unit had been during the Battle of the Bulge. I thought revisiting the landscape where these events had transpired would trigger more memories and provide new stories. Cues can improve recall if they provide a match in some way with how the memory of an event was stored. We entered the Ardennes forest from Germany at a small border crossing and travelled the roads that information in the war diaries of his unit suggested were the ones he likely travelled along. In general, being in the area some forty-five years later did not evoke more, or clearer, memories for my father. However, when we drove down a winding road into the valley toward the village of Niederwampach and crossed a bridge, he had me stop the vehicle to point out that it had been beside that bridge where he had driven his machine into the river to wash it off after unloading the wounded and dying soldiers he had picked up after they had been shelled.

Although it might have been the inexperience of a commander that was to blame for the shelling experienced by Johann's unit, it might also have been Hitler's insistence that Bastogne be captured and his refusal to authorize a retreat of any of the forces concentrated there. Hitler finally relented and allowed the withdrawal of some forces from the Bastogne area on 8 January.[23] On 14 January, after firing its last ammunition, the 5th Battalion withdrew from the Bastogne area and, like the rest of the Volks Artillerie Korps (mot.) 401, travelled back to the rear areas for rest and refit.[24]

A day or two after the corps arrived in its rest area, orders arrived with notifications of new appointments, awarding of medals, and lists of replacements. The orders of the day noted that the corps received a new commander on 4 January, a few days before the shelling that figured so prominently in my father's memory occurred and that they had blamed on an inexperienced commander. In stark contrast to what was actually happening on the battlefield, the new commander exuded extreme Nazi confidence in his letter to the troops when they arrived in the rear:

Volks-Art. Korps (mot.) 401   Battle Situation, 17.1.1945
—Kommandeur—
Volks-Art. Korps—Orders of the Day
Comrades!

As of 4.1.1945, I have taken over command of the Volks-Art. Korps (mot.) 401.

With proud joy, I have heard about your engagements and successes from both the Army Group and Army. I am proud to be the leader of such an artillery corps.

I am of the firm belief that you will continue to do your duty, despite the burdens of responsibility [*Belastungen*] and the difficult weather [*Witterungsunbilden*].

With fanatic belief in Germany's victory and unshakable loyalty to the Führer, we will fight and destroy our enemy.

Victory is still ours!

Long live the Führer.
[signature illegible][25]

Among the medals announced when they were preparing for their next engagement was an Iron Cross 2nd Class for Milostav Zacharda, Johann's long-term friend, when judged by soldiers' standards, and whom my father had remembered as Zachada Miller.[26]

After two weeks of rest, the corps was again on the move from its rest areas to the west side of the Rhine River near Koblenz. The movement of vehicles and cannons took from 5 to 10 February. From there, the corps received immediate orders to entrain and was transported to the area around Xanten just west of the Rhine before it crosses into The Netherlands, arriving there on 17 February. To prepare for the unit's reinsertion into battle, twenty-two replacements filled its depleted ranks.[27]

Most entries in the war diary of this period refer only to constant repositioning of the batteries. On 18 and 19 February, the 5th Battalion was in Luisendorf; on 20 February, it moved to the Sportspalast; and on 21 February, it moved to the area around Behrens. On 22 February, the battalion moved to Nabershof, where it remained through 25 February. At each location, the diarist reported that the battalion was ready to fire, but it seems that the pressures of battle prevented reporting the kind of detail present in the earlier entries. On 28 February and 1 March, the tross was moved to Rheinberg. On 2 March, a major move occurred, with all the support vehicles and as many Zugmaschines as possible being moved across the Rhine River. The batteries remained in the narrow strip of land left to the Germans west of the Rhine to be what the diarist referred to as the Schwerpunkt Artillerie in the bridgehead. The diary entries reflect the battles of the Reichswald, described by military historians as the scene of bitter fighting.[28]

After crossing the Rhine River, a vivid memory for my father, the 401 reassembled on 8 March near Peddenberg and then went into firing positions on the banks of the Rhine south of Wesel. An indication of the deteriorating German military capability was the command for battalions to establish communication line patrols to walk the lines every two hours with the order to shoot anyone found sabotaging them. On 9 March, new orders were received, and "after refuelling and travelling in bad weather" the 401 spent 11 March driving to Etten, just north of the border in The Netherlands.[29]

The availability of daily diaries offered a complementary narrative for the stories my father told when I formally interviewed him. He never saw the diaries, which I received while my formal interviews with him were taking place. Compared with the daily accounts in the diaries, his stories were even more disconnected from the larger events of the war but also from the immediate military objectives in which he took part. His stories expanded and contracted time and often failed to distinguish among various periods of markedly different activities as recorded in the war diaries. For instance, he made almost no distinction between periods of rest and refit and combat. In his stories, these periods merged, and it seemed as if the entire period between November 1944 and the end of the war was one long period of combat. The war diaries record eight actual days of combat engagement in the Saar region, about two weeks in the Ardennes, and approximately two weeks in the Rhine-crossing battles. My father had few clearly demarcated stories of the rest of the time, which he likely spent waiting, repairing equipment, and running errands. On occasion, when something out of the ordinary happened, such as the soldiers hanging from trees at the edge of the road, or the incident in the Dutch farmer's barn, he was apparently not in battle, but for the most part he had no stories of the day-to-day events of these times of disengagement.

Remembering and telling, as I have done in this chapter, produce an account that is not my father's story, or mine, or that of the war diaries but some combination of all of them. Geoffrey Cubitt suggests that stories of our past can be of a number of kinds: "an account of things that is coherent, or that commands general assent, ...or that minimizes friction, or that enhances self esteem, or that legitimizes certain claims or structures of authority."[30] Most listeners to my father's stories, while they might recognize them in these pages, would soon also conclude that they acquired a significantly different texture after the collaboration of a number of alternative ways of telling that produced this account.

The Collapse

THE PUSH TO CROSS THE RHINE RIVER in northern Germany by General Montgomery's armies began in earnest on 23 March 1945. The 401's 5th Battalion diarist recorded that at 4:00 p.m. the enemy was creating a smoke-screen along the entire front and that at 5:00 p.m. a "drum roll" artillery barrage began. Military histories would later note that by 8:00 p.m. that evening 3,500 guns were firing to prepare for the Rhine crossing.[1] The Allies soon had a bridgehead at Wesel, and the 401 was forced to move, first to Dorsten, then north of the Lippe Canal, which ran parallel to the Lippe River. My father's account of trying to stay ahead of the advancing Allied offensive conveyed the sense of confusion and danger that gripped the remnants of the Wehrmacht.

When they crossed from Holland into Germany, they had to cross a small river. The bridge had been damaged, so they had to drive through the water in the dark. The artillery shelling was behind them but coming ever closer. When Johann got to the river, there was no option but to go through it. My father thought he must have been going quite fast because the front of the machine went under water, but when it straightened out it was just above water enough to keep going, even though water was coming in under the doors. When he had trouble getting up the far bank, he applied all the power the machine had to get up the bank. He drove for some time before stopping, and when he did someone came running up to thank him for pulling him through the river. Johann had not realized that someone had hooked his truck to his machine before he entered the river.[2]

In another account, my father described their arrival in a forest, where it seemed they would attempt to hold their position. They were soon on the move again and driving over flooded areas due to Allied bombing of a dam.[3] In his recollection, they crossed over into Germany after driving the last distance through water. The British, or Americans, he could not remember which, had seen them drive their machines with the cannons into the forest, and they were soon bombarded with phosphorus bombs. Two of their machines went up in smoke (though Johann's machine and its cannons were spared), one soldier's clothes were burned, and while the flames lit the forest on fire there was hardly any underbrush to really fuel it. Although they could drive, my father noted they could not go far because by this time they were surrounded in what was called the Ruhr pocket.[4]

Desperate measures were taken, but a dismal sight greeted them as Johann's unit was pushed farther into Germany. Civilians were being pressed into fighting roles in a last-ditch attempt to defend their cities with whatever was available. Hitler had dubbed this effort the "Volkssturm"—literally the "people's storm." When Johann's unit entered Germany from Holland, it came across a scene of old men being assembled to defend the country; "they were between fifty-five and sixty-five." The absolute devastation that surrounded them prompted one of Johann's fellow soldiers to remark that Hitler had always said "*Sonnige und luftige Wohnungen sollt ihr haben*" ("You shall have sunny and airy homes") and claim that, "Now we have them!"[5]

In the confusion of retreat, some of the battalions became separated from the others, and they lost contact with each other as the German front collapsed. Johann's 2nd Battalion ended up being pushed south into the Ruhr industrial area, while the 5th Battalion went north to fight for another month until Germany finally capitulated. Johann lost his Zugmaschine because airplanes found it whenever he left the forest. He received a new twelve-tonne Zugmaschine, his third, while they were already surrounded by the Allies. The end of the war came quietly for Johann.

On 11 April, he left Unna to go to Dortmund to pick up vehicles for repair. The vehicles were the shoemaker's truck with its crew of four shoemakers and the truck of the tailor who repaired the uniforms. Johann hitched them together to follow his machine because the trucks no longer had their drivers, and the cobbler and tailor did not know how to drive. On the way back, when Johann was about twenty kilometres from Unna, a dark object loomed ahead on the road, and someone signalled with a flashlight. By this time, as my father put it, "everybody knew that at any time we would be captured, or we would die, one of the two, there was no other alternative." Johann had already removed his helmet because it was too hot and the belt with his pistol so as not to be confused with someone who still wanted to fight. When they realized that the moment had come, he and his companions calmly surrendered. They were taken to Unna in a jeep, and "our entire company was there—all prisoners, even our officer, everyone had surrendered." When the officer called the roll, only four members of the unit were unaccounted for. He released the unit to the Americans "on the condition that the promises they made in their propaganda leaflets that those who gave themselves up without shooting would receive better treatment than others."[6] The war had finally come to an end for Johann.

We tell our life experiences using the tools of narrative, including turning points to mark where we want to convey major changes in the directions of our lives—what Frank Kermode calls the "point from which all can be seen to cohere, and so achieves a kind of closure."[7] One would think that 11 April 1945, the day my father was captured, would have been such a day—it was not. The war was over for Johann, but the dying continued.

In my father's memory, the soldiers who initially guarded him and his fellow prisoners were all African American: "they were not very polite, they tore up the pictures you had and ground them in the dirt; they were very rough." In my memories of the stories my father told, I seem to recall him saying they were then put in large fenced-in enclosures for a while before being shipped off to France. The US Army established large enclosures on the east side of the Rhine River where they collected the large numbers of prisoners captured in the last months of the war. These camps, known as Rhinewiesenlager, were rudimentary and overcrowded. Here my reading of Second World War history might be creating my own false memory. In the taped interviews with my father, and in a further conversation with him after I did more research, he maintained that he was immediately loaded onto a train and taken to France.

He and many other captured German soldiers were packed into steel rail cars at the Unna train station, about forty soldiers per car. Some prisoners were loaded into open cars, but the one that Johann was in was completely closed. My father recalled that POWs who travelled in the open cars had things thrown at them when they passed under bridges in France, and he heard rocks hitting the roof of the car he was in. Their transport to France turned out to be on unusually hot days, and somewhere between the Ruhr area and their destination east of

Paris the oxygen in the car seemed to disappear. There were no windows, they could not see what was going on, and it was getting terribly hot. Johann was in the front corner of the car, where one of the floorboards was damaged, so he was able to get fresh air through the opening in the floor. He sat there motionless taking in the fresh air. Around him, however, the soldiers were panicking: "they were cursing and moving around, the sweat was running down." Someone managed to pry a board loose, and the soldiers used it to smash a hole in the roof of the car to get some air. The U.S. soldiers, patrolling on the roofs of the train cars, thought an escape was being attempted and fired into the hole with their machine guns: "there was blood and everything all over." Seven soldiers died, and a number of others were wounded. The train did not stop. The incident took place in the afternoon, but the train continued through Luxembourg toward Paris before it arrived at its destination the next day. The less seriously wounded were "bandaged, and we applied tourniquets, some of them stayed alive, but some of them died."[8]

The train unloaded its human cargo at a place my father called "my little camp"—at least that is how I understood it. Given that he had been under American guard and never acquired a good command of English, that was how it sounded; as he said, "what that means I do not know to this day." The camp was on a hill, he recalled, and probably sixty kilometres from Paris. He thought there were 48,000 POWs in the camp, the same number he had used for the mass of male humanity in the camps on the eastern front, where he had been captured by the Germans in 1941. Arrival at the camp meant they were now in French hands. They were whipped as they entered the camp by what my father believed were Jews but could have been French guards avenging themselves against their German occupiers. They had to strip to the waist and raise their arms for inspection so that the blood type tattoo that marked SS members could be detected and they could be separated from the others. The Wehrmacht soldiers quipped that "before they [the SS] had always been the first, they might as well be first now."[9]

Conditions in the camp were horrible. It was out in the open, with no shelter from rain or wind. The latrine was a hole in the ground with a board across it. There was not enough food, and the weakest of the soldiers fainted while relieving themselves and drowned in their own excrement. A truck that drove to the edge of the camp just outside the wire fence provided water by pouring it into the enclosure from a hose. Prisoners fought each other to get water. Every day trucks came to load up dead bodies.

Johann had been in the camp for a few weeks when the Red Cross came to inspect it in the morning, before the dead had been picked up. The camp was then taken over by the Americans, who provided adequate food, but the dramatic increase in the amount of food caused more deaths. Prisoners consumed too much food too quickly despite the warnings of doctors among them. A call for prisoners who had a valid driver's licence was Johann's ticket out. The U.S. Army was assembling a group of prisoners to clean up ammunition stockpiled in the French countryside and needed drivers who were also mechanics. Johann volunteered since he had managed to keep his German driver's licence.[10]

Some ten years after my father told me these stories, a Quebec novelist published a controversial account of the treatment of German POWs at the end of the Second World War.[11] James Bacque's book *Other Losses* was widely rejected by historians. His thesis was that Eisenhower deliberately allowed a million German POWs to die of starvation because he hated Germans. Bacque was accused of misreading documents, ignoring evidence that did not support his thesis, and using statistical methodology that was "hopelessly compromised." In his review of Bacque's book, Steven Ambrose, Eisenhower's biographer, grudgingly admitted, however, that "there was widespread mistreatment of German prisoners in the spring and summer of 1945" and that "men did die needlessly and inexcusably."[12] It was almost surreal to read *Other Losses* and related sources. I realized that my father's reference to "my little camp" was the POW camp at Maily-le-Camp, about 220 kilometres east of Paris. On 16 March 1945, a month or more before the events my father described, 120 German prisoners were found dead on trains that arrived there. They had suffocated in their tightly sealed train cars. Directives were issued to correct these problems, and according to Bacque, Eisenhower reluctantly issued an apology. It seems, however, that the problem of poorly ventilated train cars with large numbers of prisoners in them was not solved quickly.[13]

At Maily-le-Camp, the enclosure adjacent to Johann's, and separated only by a barbed wire fence, was filled with Ukrainians and Russians. The Germans had forcibly moved workers from occupied areas of the Soviet Union to work as virtual slave labourers in German factories. It was these *ostarbeiter* and remnants of the Vlasov Army, former Red Army soldiers whom the Nazis had recruited to fight Bolshevism, who had been assembled next to the prisoners of war at Maily-le-Camp. Early in his stay there, Johann frequently talked to the soldiers, who encouraged him to come over to their enclosure because he spoke Russian and because they received better rations. He declined the offer, suggesting that he "had been treated as a German while in Russia" and had no desire to go back there. One day it seemed that preparations were being made to send them back to the Soviet Union, and Johann went over to talk to them, advising them not to return, especially not those who had served in the Vlasov Army. But they were excited to be going home, back to their families. Johann volunteered to help prepare the train cars on which they were to be transported; it was an opportunity to get out a little. The train was decorated with evergreen branches and the hammer and sickle emblem of the Soviet Union. Each car got an allocation of ten boxes of K-rations, enough for two days of travel for twenty or so people in one car. When the train left, an American officer commented that they had just experienced their last moment of joy, suggesting he knew more about their fate than they were being told. Two trains had left when four of the Vlasov Army soldiers from the second train showed up again at the camp. They described the sudden change as soon as they had crossed into the Soviet-controlled zone of Germany. Soviet soldiers had opened the train cars, accused them of being traitors, and told them they would be sent to Siberia or shot as soon as the train was on Soviet territory. The four men who had returned had been in one car and managed to break the floorboards, so that the entire group of twenty had escaped. These four were the only ones who had made it back; Soviet guards had recaptured the rest. The return of the Russians caused quite a stir in the camp, and the remaining Russians and Ukrainians refused repatriation. They went to the American commanders and pleaded with them not to force their repatriation to the Soviet Union. Thereafter, it seemed that only those who wanted to go back left the camp. Soviet officials, however, were still allowed into the camp to attempt to repatriate their citizens. On one occasion, camp inmates overturned their vehicle when it entered the camp, and military police had to intervene.[14]

Volunteering to join a group of prisoners to clean up ammunition was Johann's salvation, though it meant that Johann and his friend Milostav Zacharda were separated. Zacharda declared himself Czechoslovakian and went home. Johann was moved to Étain, France, just west of Metz, not far from where his unit had first fought in the Saar battles six months earlier. Two POW camps were located in the area. His group of truck drivers stayed in barracks inside the town where they were properly fed; about six kilometres away was another camp with barracks. They picked up prisoners of war at the other camp just outside Étain who loaded and unloaded the trucks and then went to clean up ammunition. They drove all over southern France, always under guard. The first task was to clean up ammunition in the area around Verdun. The roadsides were piled high with ammunition, enough that my father thought there were sufficient shells "to fight a war for another five years." The ammunition was piled as high as their trucks on both sides of the road for twenty or thirty kilometres. Their task was to load the ammunition for delivery to the train station where it was shipped to harbours in the south of France. Damaged ammunition was collected in large pits. The shells were slid down planks into pits as large as a house, and with forty trucks hauling shells it took all week to fill three holes. On Saturdays, the pits were detonated, and my father remembered the resulting explosion being "like an atomic bomb." On one occasion, when the wind was from the wrong direction, windows in the town some fifty kilometres away were blown out, and the U.S. Army had to replace them.[15]

The POWs that Johann and his fellow drivers picked up at the other camp were under French administration and poorly fed. On one occasion, they came upon six POWs who were near starvation and unable to work. Johann's group asked their guards whether they could deliver excess food to the other prison camp and were given permission to do so, but guards had to accompany them when they entered the camp because of the turmoil that ensued among prisoners eager to get to the food.[16]

Some prisoners saw the work of loading and unloading ammunition as an opportunity to escape. Once, when they became aware that the train they were loading was headed for Munich, they left an opening among the shells large enough for six of them to hide. With the assistance of others, they hid in the opening with some rations they had stored and had others conceal them with the rest of the shells. Some POWs who knew them later received letters from them telling of their escape. When they had heard only German spoken while stopped at a train station, they had left the cars and gone home.[17]

Once the ammunition work was done, Johann's group of drivers transported supplies for the occupation army. Early every morning the convoy of 200 to 300 trucks left for the port of Marseilles in the south of France to pick up supplies and bring them to supply bases in Metz and Rheims before returning to their barracks at Étain late in the evening. They had to wear uniforms with a large "P" on one knee and shoulder and a "W" on the other. They were issued three sets of these uniforms, which Johann thought looked quite sharp. French civilians often thought they were American soldiers and were friendly to them, at least until they found out what "PW" stood for.[18]

Johann was finally scheduled to be released in the summer of 1946, but because of concerns for their safety the group of drivers he had worked with were to be released in Regensburg in the American zone. They were transported in a special train and housed in the former Messerschmitt factories, now converted to temporary barracks. When the American officials in Regensburg found out they were a group of prisoners who had specialized in cleaning up ammunition, they were held there for a few weeks longer to clean up a pile of munitions left by the Germans in the forest near Munich. The abandoned piles of shells were dangerous, and no one wanted to touch them, but prisoners of war could not refuse. Many POWs at Regensburg were SS soldiers, and they were to be used as labour for loading and unloading, while Johann and his fellow POWs were to be the drivers, as they had been in France. The difference was that a Polish guard always accompanied them; the entire camp guard contingent was Polish, likely members of the Polish Army who had served with the Allies under British command. The area was a mess of live and defective shells. Once a guard decided to have a smoke despite Johann's warnings that it was too dangerous. When he tossed his still lit cigarette into the grass, it immediately ignited. Johann and the others ran as fast as they could to find cover behind some tree stumps, and not long after the spilled powder began to ignite, followed closely by the explosions of shells on the truck. Johann and the others had to run farther into the forest as the intensity of the heat set the whole pile of ammunition off. Shrapnel injured a few of the POWs and killed the Polish guard, who had waited too long before leaving. When U.S. Army personnel heard the explosions, fire trucks came and eventually extinguished the flames. Three trucks had been completely destroyed. Johann and his fellow POWs told the Americans they wanted to do their work without guards, as they had done in France. Consequently the Polish guards were taken away, and Johann's group continued cleaning up ammunition without guards.

The war was not easily forgotten by those who had suffered atrocities at the hands of the Nazis, particularly those who had been victims of the SS in Eastern Europe. In the immediate postwar climate, the desire for revenge could not always be controlled. Just before Johann was released after returning to Regensburg, he watched a soccer game on a Sunday between the SS POWs and Jahn Regensburg, the city's soccer team. The game was played in the POW camp, with the field separated from the barbed wire by a ditch. During the game, the ball rolled into the ditch, and one SS player ran to fetch it, forgetting the ditch was off limits. A guard in the watchtower fired at him, and he was killed. The SS POWs were sure the guard was Polish, and the incident fuelled their simmering hatred of Poles. The SS claimed "they would kill the first ten Poles they came across" after their release. The Polish guards gathered signatures from other prisoners to prove they had treated the POWs decently. My father maintained that he "had only been there a few weeks; we didn't know anything about what had all happened before we arrived. We all saw this, and it was terrible."[19] The Polish guard was removed from his post and imprisoned. After about sixty or seventy SS prisoners were later released, word got back to the camp that a Polish man had been thrown off a bridge over the Danube River.

Once Johann and his comrades got to the actual release process, things went quickly though not without tensions. Before being released, Johann had to appear before another panel made up of Soviet, British, French, and American officials. He was asked to which zone he wanted to be released and chose the American one. The Soviet official asked why he did not want to be released to East Prussia, since according to his documentation he had been born there. The question created a moment of anxiety for Johann, but he answered that he wanted to stay in the Regensburg area.

The story of his release, along with the earlier story of his encounter with Russians and Ukrainians who were being repatriated, illustrated most clearly the complete separation from his former life in the Soviet Union. In my formal interviews, I asked my father at this point whether he had ever considered going back.

No, there was no chance, for me it was impossible. It was possible—

Yes, but you knew, and were completely convinced, that if you would go to Russia they would just shoot you.

Oh, yes, even the Germans said that. They told me they would not send me to the eastern front because, if the Russians got hold of me, they would shoot me. There were only a few Russians in German prison camps, and if they escaped the Russians didn't accept them, they were spies to them, they just shot them. They were crazy, plain crazy. Almost nobody believes you—the American prisoners of war were given a heroes' welcome when they came home; the same for the Germans. And for the Russians, they were all killed, or he [Stalin] put them in jail for ten years.[20]

My father's stories about his prisoner-of-war camp experiences marked the culmination of a change in his identity that had begun with his capture by the Germans in 1941. His stories portrayed Poles and Jews in a negative light, probably much like the attitudes prevalent among the Germans who had become his comrades, but they were a change from his stories of living in occupied Poland in 1942 and 1943. There was still animosity toward the SS, not unlike the attitudes that pervaded the ranks of ordinary Wehrmacht soldiers, and his aversion to the Soviet system had become complete. His stories conveyed the absolute closure that Johann had made with the Soviet past, even though he was alone, had no home in the West, and had no connections to his earlier life. Surprisingly, perhaps, Americans were treated favourably in his stories. Although they fed him poorly, shot some of his fellow prisoners, and were sometimes abusive and disrespectful, Johann still wanted to be released in the American zone. In that sense, his personal story came to be framed in Cold War terms, much like the master narrative of "us and them" that quickly came to be the dominant narrative of the postwar period. Nazism faded into the past, and the new ideological enemy, the Soviet Union, emerged as the archrival.

PART 3

Becoming Normal

New Beginnings

ON 21 AUGUST 1946, Johann obtained his freedom, and the war was finally over for him. His release was a turning point. As my father later put it in his stories, "after many years of being in the army, then in a prison camp, now finally you were a free person—and you didn't know what you were supposed to do with yourself." For ten years, he had always had orders, and his choices, while often important for survival, had been circumscribed by war, armies, and the commands of others. He was twenty-eight years old and had lost much. He had no home, his mother and siblings were on the other side of what Winston Churchill earlier that spring had called the "iron curtain," he had left behind a wife in Siberia both emotionally and physically, and he knew nothing about what had happened to any of them.[1]

His stories about the next few years changed. They were on a different scale. As David Thelan notes, "the difference between personal memory and history is one of scale."[2] The end of the war marked the end of stories in which my father took an active part, albeit a small part, in large-scale and momentous events. After his release from the POW camp, his world and his stories were about the rhythms of work, primary relationships, and the everyday.

Johann was released together with a prisoner whom he had known for some time and who also did not want to go home because he was from East Prussia, now under Soviet control. The two made their way to the Regensburg train station. They had received a railway pass good for four weeks of travel anywhere in Germany. They had also received ration cards that allowed them to eat at Red Cross stations anywhere. But they did not know where to go. They stayed in Regensburg for two nights, discussed what they should do, and talked to people they met about their plight. An older man advised them to go to Bamberg, which was not far away and had not been badly bombed during the war. It had a few factories, and he thought they might have a chance at a job. The next day they headed for Bamberg, where Johann saw trucks passing by with a familiar symbol on their doors, a round chain with an exploding bomb in the middle, the same symbol that had been on the trucks they had driven as prisoners of the Americans. He pointed out the trucks to his friend and suggested they follow them. They noted the direction they were heading, and at the end of the street they entered a large compound, a former panzer or artillery *kaserne.* They told the guard at the gate they were looking for work; he called someone who took them to the office. Sitting at the desk was the same commander Johann had worked for in France. He recognized him immediately, and when they asked about a job he offered Johann work on the spot because they were in desperate need of qualified truck drivers. The commander asked about his friend, who was not a truck driver, and offered him work in the mess.

They had both achieved an important beginning, a job, but they had no place to live. The commander mentioned that each day they picked up a group of workers from a nearby camp and offered to phone and check if they could live there as well. Luck was on their side again, and in the evening the truck came by, and the two of them went to their new home at Weide 28. It was a refugee camp, and they slept in one huge room together with at least 100 other people. There were rows and rows of beds with aisles between them, and one had to be careful to find one's own bed. They used their ration cards to get breakfast, and their "new" employer provided the other two meals. In my father's telling of this story, his new job was driving a truck on a long-distance route, from Bamberg to Hamburg in northern Germany. It was an International semi truck, and a U.S. Army MP was always beside Johann. He was armed, and when they stopped to eat either Johann or the MP always stayed with the truck because it was loaded with luxury goods: watches, rings, cigarettes, and chocolate. These goods were being transported to the PX department store where American military personnel shopped. The documents of his employment during this time suggest that his first job was with the 3492nd Ordnance MAM Company. On 17 January 1947, Johann was transferred to the Army Post Office, where he also worked as a driver.[3]

Other new beginnings followed. One day he and a helper were working beneath his truck repairing the transmission. When the wrench his helper was using slipped out of his hand and hit him on the head, he swore in Low German, though the way my father told it he uttered "a few Mennonite words, very unusual Mennonite words." When Johann asked him about the Low German expression he had used, the helper claimed to be from Poland, but after further conversation in Low German they both came out with the truth. He was not from Poland, and Johann was not from East Prussia; they were both Mennonites from Russia. As far as my father could remember, his last name was Heinrichs.[4] His new acquaintance told him there were about eighty Mennonites meeting together for worship in Bamberg and invited Johann to join them. They met in the same space as the Baptists, with one group holding services on Sunday morning and the other Sunday evening. The next Sunday Johann attended a Mennonite worship service, probably for the first time in his life. The other Mennonites were a little perplexed at his name, since the Werner surname was uncommon among Russian Mennonites. However, his fluency in Low German sealed his identity—he was clearly Mennonite. The leader of the small group was a man by the name of Wiebe who also asked if he had any relatives in Canada. When Johann told him he had a sister there, Wiebe assured him he could emigrate to Canada, a prospect that had been the furthest thing from his mind until that point. The small group of Mennonites provided a new and interesting social, though seemingly not religious, awakening in Johann. He got to know the Heinrichs, who had two small children, and was a frequent guest in their home.

My father's stories of that time centred on work, but there was also time for recreation and visiting. Johann skied in Garmisch–Partenkirchen in the Alps and had fond memories of attending the New Year's celebrations at the castle on the hill just outside Bamberg. It was during this time that he visited Schneider's family in Wurzburg. Little in his stories concerned persons with whom he became friends or the daily life of the refugee camp where he lived.

The long trips to Hamburg with the truck did not occupy all of his working time; Johann often made only one trip a week, sometimes less. Since he was assigned to the Bamberg Military Sub Post motor pool, he had other driving assignments.[5] One was to chauffeur two lawyers involved in the Nuremberg war crimes trials. Since they spoke no German and he no English, there was little conversation on the way to the trials. Johann took them to Nuremberg from Bamberg, a distance of about sixty kilometres, and then spent the day in the area of the trial building reserved for drivers and other support staff. The room was a kind of gallery with windows that looked down over the proceedings and with a sound system that enabled them to hear everything going on. According to his stories, my father was present when Hermann Goering told the court they would not hang him, and he was there when the defendants made their final statements.[6] Although he was likely present for portions of the last few weeks of the trials, his account seemed to intermingle what he had heard and seen with newspaper accounts of the events, which were widely reported. My father seemed to hint at this in his interview when he acknowledges that "it was reported every day in the newspapers."[7]

The casual comment made by the leader of the small Mennonite group he had joined in Bamberg that having a sister in Canada would make emigration possible did not end there. Wiebe was one of what were called *vertrauensmänner*, a refugee appointed as a contact person for a local area by the Mennonite Central Committee (MCC). It was a North American relief organization that worked hard to gather the remnants of Mennonite refugees who had managed to stay ahead of Soviet armies and were scattered throughout the western zones of occupied Germany. In Canada, the work of resettling refugees was taken up by another organization, the Canadian Mennonite Board of Colonization (CMBC). Wiebe assisted Johann in contacting the MCC to try to find his sister in Canada. In a letter dated 2 May 1948 addressed to the Board of Colonization and signed by Johann, but otherwise not in his handwriting, he requested assistance in locating his sister. In his memory of these events, my father was not sure what "Steinbach" or "Manitoba" might be, but he remembered those two words in connection with her address. In the letter, he outlined details of himself and what he knew about his sister. He noted that he was single, mentioned that he had been born in Nikolaipol, and provided details about his parents. He mentioned his uncle Aaron Janzen, who had migrated to Canada in 1925, and his sister, Aganetha Werner, who was married at the time of writing but had emigrated from Silberfeld as the foster child of Aaron. The letter did not mention Steinbach as a possible address. It was sent via the MCC to the CMBC offices in Saskatoon, Saskatchewan, and within a few days they responded. In a letter dated 20 May 1948, Johann was advised that they had located both his sister and his uncle in Steinbach and that his uncle was being notified of his whereabouts.[8] Johann seemingly did not take immediate action on emigration, but early in 1949 he was granted a leave of absence from his job to travel to begin the process.

A myriad of agencies and bureaucracies had to be navigated before ethnic German emigrants such as Johann boarded the ship at Bremerhaven headed for Quebec City or Halifax. Documents from his workplace suggest he was gone from 31 January to 10 February 1949, probably for a preliminary visit to the MCC offices. A few months later the seemingly unending process of trying to leave Germany began in earnest. He quit his job with the U.S. Army on 23 March and travelled to the MCC refugee camp in Backnang in southwest Germany for processing.[9]

After a few days in Backnang, Johann was sent to Ludwigsburg to appear before the International Refugee Organization (IRO). The IRO was a UN organization charged with resettling displaced persons (DPs) in Europe after the war, though the Soviet Union ultimately did not participate. Canada accepted large numbers of DPs from a variety of nationalities as part of a humanitarian effort to alleviate the refugee problem in Europe. While in Backnang, Johann asked the MCC secretary, Marie Brunk, which questions he would be asked when he appeared before IRO officials. She indicated that he would not be granted IRO status if he had received German ration cards, if he had become a German citizen, or if he had served in the German military. Johann protested he had done all of them, but Brunk suggested he appear anyway to see what would happen. He took the hour-long train ride to Ludwigsburg, where he appeared before an IRO official who spoke perfect Russian.[10] The official asked Johann if he had been in the Red Army and whether he had been captured by the Germans. He replied yes to both questions, whereupon the officer tested his knowledge of Russian, stamped his documents, declared him to be stateless, and granted him IRO status.

The next step was to go to the IRO resettlement camp at Fallingbostel to be processed for emigration by other agencies. As one MCC worker described it, Fallingbostel was "an insignificant little village in northern Germany, not much more than a wide place in the rough cobblestone road." Just outside the village in a scenic spot in the landscape was a large former German military base used by the IRO to process refugees.[11] The MCC had a presence in the camp and assisted Mennonite refugees who were eligible for IRO status.

Although seemingly having been granted IRO status, on 23 April 1949 Johann received word that his application to emigrate to Canada had been rejected by the Combined Travel Board, an organization of Allied occupying forces that controlled travel between zones, including granting permission to those wanting to leave Germany. The reason for his rejection was that Johann was a German citizen.[12] The IRO considered the rejection temporary, with the MCC staff person noting that according "to the local IRO staff person—Miss Taylor—the case is not entirely closed."[13] Upon his rejection by the Combined Travel Board, the MCC pursued its second option, having Johann processed through another organization, the Canadian Christian Council for the Resettlement of Refugees (outside the mandate of the IRO), the CCCRR.

The reduced travel costs if a potential immigrant, or PI as they came to be labelled in the documents, was given IRO status meant that it became the preferred method of processing. If that was unsuccessful, the MCC and other religious organizations such as Lutheran World Relief and Baptist World Alliance used the CCCRR, an organization they had created specifically for the purpose of bringing to Canada ethnic Germans who were outside the IRO's mandate.

The form that the MCC required Johann to fill out when he applied to emigrate reveals a lot about who he considered himself to be. Under the section on religion and church affiliation, he indicated that he was not baptized but belonged to the Kirchengemeinde rather than the Mennonite Brethren Church. He indicated that he did not regularly attend a Mennonite church but believed himself to be Mennonite because his parents had been Mennonite. He thought, however, that it would be possible for him to attend a Mennonite church regularly. He indicated that he had a job and earned a salary of 180 DM per month but was unhappy with his housing arrangements. A curiously worded question asked if he was prepared to emigrate at all costs, to which he replied he was because "of fear of the Communists" and gave as a second reason the fact that he had a sister in Canada. He indicated that he had been accepted by the IRO at Nellingen. The questionnaire again hinted at untold stories about his relationships. He reported his marital status as single, not divorced, and with no children born out of wedlock. He indicated, however, that he was engaged but prepared to emigrate even if his fiancée could not.

Surprisingly Johann denied having become a German citizen.[14] In difficult cases, the MCC asked potential emigrants to make a statement that included a biography and specifically addressed concerns that had arisen in their processing. The "story" that Johann told after being rejected by the Combined Travel Board was a version of the events of his stay in the Warthegau during the interlude between his service in the armies of Stalin and Hitler.

> I, Johann Werner, was born on January 6, 1917, in Markow, Siberia. I attended elementary school for seven years and did farm work until 1939.

> In 1939, I was drafted into the Russian Army. In June 1941, I was taken a prisoner of war by the Germans in Grodnau [sic], Poland.

> The German officers frequently came into our camp to persuade the POWs to volunteer for the German Army. However, I was sick of war and did not volunteer. I was kept a prisoner of war by the Germans until October 1944, when I was released to be drafted against my will into the German Army, at Angerab [sic], East Prussia.

> I was drafted into the 401st motorized artillery division. When the Russians overtook our division near Berlin, I fled and was taken a prisoner of war by the Americans on April 11, 1945, near Dortmund, Germany. I was imprisoned in France until my release in August 1946.

> I have been recently informed that I was naturalized as a German citizen in October 1942. This was news to me! At that time, I was being held as a prisoner of war by the Germans. I never made a request to be naturalized. Neither do I recall ever having completed any documents that might have been the request for naturalization—as such things were sometimes [done] by the Germans without our knowledge. Other POWs received naturalization certificates, but I never received such a document.

> Signed Johann Werner[15]

Stories are told for different purposes and for different audiences. There are significant elements of this version of my father's biography that are clearly fabrications to try to gain permission to emigrate, not uncommon for men with "spoilt" biographies in the disrupted world of war-torn Europe. As historian Ted Regehr concludes, the cherished Mennonite values of truth and honesty "may appear differently to people in complex, difficult and morally ambiguous situations."[16] The MCC struggled constantly with the problem of people whom it considered co-religionists who had not been entirely honest and whom, for humanitarian reasons, it was trying to help escape from the grip of Stalin. In one memo, the director of the Gronau MCC office, Siegfried Janzen, detailed a number of difficult cases to his counterpart in Fallingbostel. Janzen noted that one prospective emigrant was asked three times if he had been in the army. The candidate lied each time until the official examined him for the telltale tattoo of SS members. When the blood mark tattoo was found, he confessed to having been not only in the army but also in the Waffen SS. In his concluding remarks, Janzen noted that, before sending this particular group of candidates to Fallingbostel, he had touched on "the matter of truthfulness" in his conversations with them.[17]

The CCCRR was also unable to get Johann's application to emigrate approved, and on 5 July 1949 Johann was transferred to the MCC's main camp at Gronau near the Dutch border in northern Germany. Things continued to go wrong. On 23 July, the IRO suspended processing of all Mennonite applicants because it had determined that many of them were German citizens and had served in the German Army. The IRO had discovered that many Mennonites, certainly Johann was a prime example, had become citizens as early as 1942 and in that sense failed one of the IRO's tests: namely, that no one who had "voluntarily assisted the enemy forces since the outbreak of the second world war in their operations against the United Nations" was eligible for IRO assistance.[18] In September, the IRO formally advised Johann that he had been rejected.[19] He continued to languish in the Gronau MCC camp while the MCC marshalled all its diplomatic and political resources to try to lift the IRO ban. According to one of my father's stories, his position became further complicated when Johann appeared at an interview just after three of his friends had appeared before officials. All three had been in the SS and had lied to the examining official. When Johann arrived, he was asked if he had also been in the SS. When he denied any involvement with it, the official accused him of lying like the others, even though he did not find the blood mark tattoo under his arm. His application was rejected.[20]

The prospect of emigrating to Canada faded away. Wading through the many documents of his attempted emigration leads one to conclude that the main obstacle preventing entry into Canada was that Johann had become a German citizen in 1942. Although the IRO ultimately considered the naturalization of Mennonites who had arrived in occupied Poland as refugees in 1943 as having come under duress, Johann's naturalization and subsequent service in the Wehrmacht were viewed as voluntary and Johann as an enemy German.

Even while his emigration attempt was failing, there were other new beginnings. While Johann was in Gronau, he met Margarethe Vogt, a Mennonite refugee from Ukraine. As she said later, she had heard Johann Werner being called over the public address system in the Gronau refugee camp and commented to others that the name seemed unusual and could not be Mennonite. My father recalled that they had agreed to go on a date, but because she had not wanted to start rumours they had agreed to meet away from prying eyes. He did not recognize her at the appointed spot because she was now dressed up, while she recalled thinking that he had stood her up.[21] Johann also formally joined the Mennonite church. Although my father never told any stories about this aspect of his re-entry into Mennonite life after the war, it seems he felt the need for a faith and an ethnic community. A distinctive feature of Mennonite faith practice is adult baptism, usually preceded by a period of study and instruction and, in the postwar context, a personal interview to determine whether the intent to join the faith was genuine or merely an attempt to be affiliated with a group that might help a person desperate to emigrate. A photo of the group that my father was baptized with and a certificate that he kept were the only evidence of this part of his story.

While in Gronau, Johann also began to work outside the camp as a welder at the Empf van Delden textile factories. However, when the MCC was preparing to close the Gronau camp in 1950, and with seemingly no prospect of emigration, Johann moved out of the camp to the town of Neuwied along the Rhine River. On 22 September 1950, he began work as a rolling mill worker at the Eisen und Hüttenwerke, a metal-working concern in Neuwied.[22] There he and some friends, most of them also former Mennonite soldiers, shared accommodations in a building on Kirchstrasse. Some were the SS friends who had caused him trouble during their processing.

Meanwhile the relationship between Johann and Margarethe Vogt blossomed. She and her parents, who also could not emigrate, had moved to Walgenbach, a small village about fifty kilometres from Neuwied. On weekends, Johann travelled to visit her, at first by bicycle and then on a BMW motorcycle he had bought. Together they made trips into the countryside on motorcycle, visited parks, and went on outings with friends.

Although emigrating was becoming less of a priority, Johann's budding relationship with Margarethe complicated that question considerably. Her

*Johann Werner (centre, third row) together with other candidates
on the occasion of his baptism in postwar Germany.*

half-sister had left for Canada in 1949, while her elderly parents, who also
wanted to emigrate, were experiencing considerable difficulty acquiring
permission to join her. But there were also developments in Canadian immigration regulations that offered new potential for Johann to emigrate.
In March 1950, the Canadian government allowed the entry of German
nationals if they were prepared to work on farms, and in September 1950 the
restriction on admission for those who had served in the German military was
lifted. By the fall of 1950, the impediments to Johann's emigration had been
removed, and the MCC contacted Johann about whether he still wanted to
emigrate to Canada. In a November 1950 letter, the MCC noted that it had
now been a year since he had been refused admission to Canada because of his
German citizenship and advised him that "naturalization is now no longer a
hindrance for going to Canada." He never responded, apparently because his
desire to emigrate was now hopelessly intertwined with Margarethe's family
and their prospects for emigration.[23] By August 1951, the relationship had
evolved into a marriage commitment. They married on 24 September 1951 in
a simple ceremony in Backnang. Gerhard Fast, a Mennonite pastor who had
known Margarethe since the end of the war, officiated.

My father's recovery from the war was reflected in the nature of his stories. The dramatic events that had been so prominent in his earlier stories were now limited to being in the gallery at the Nuremberg trials. Most of his stories lacked the kind of detail that my father remembered so vividly in his war stories. Re-entry into the everyday must have involved considerable emotional and psychological reorientation, but emotions were not typically expressed in his stories and did not appear here either. Most details of the complicated process of obtaining permission to emigrate could only be gleaned from a careful reading of documentary records. For both emigration and courting purposes, his stories had to be narrated in new ways. As his short biography for the MCC indicates, some of his past did not fit with these requirements, and a new narrative emerged, if only temporarily.

Margarethe (Sara) Vogt (Letkeman)

MARGARETHE VOGT, WHO WOULD BECOME MY MOTHER, had her own stories to tell. They offer another perspective on many of the events that my father lived through: famine, collectivization, war, and the loss of home and family. Her experience was that of a refugee, not an initiator of military actions but the recipient of the trauma they inflicted. She told her stories from the point of view of a daughter, young woman, and mother. They were more emotional, never neutral in tone, and frequently imbued with a sharper sense of the contest of values into which circumstances thrust her. At about the same time as I interviewed my father, I also interviewed her. He was present for these interviews, which necessarily coloured how she told her stories.

Little Sara Letkeman, who eventually became Margarethe and Johann's wife, was born on 13 August 1921 at the height of a famine brought on by the revolution and civil war that created the Soviet state and at the time the Werner family was almost wiped out by a cholera epidemic in Siberia. She was born in Osterwick in the heart of the Mennonite Chortitza colony beside the Dnieper River, near the present-day Ukrainian city of Zaporozhye. Her parents were Jacob and Katharina Letkeman. Her father's marriage to Katharina was his first, but for her mother it was a second marriage after the death of her first husband, a man with the surname Dyck. It meant that Sara had a half-sister, Katharina Dyck, who was seven years her senior, and when she was three and a half years old a brother, Jacob, was born. Her father was fifty when she was born; her mother was thirty-seven. The small farm they had was a shared enterprise between Jacob Letkeman and his brother Peter, and, while not the poorest in the village, they were hardly wealthy by pre-revolution Mennonite standards.

The family survived the 1921 famine because they took dishes that Sara's mother had inherited to the city to sell them to buy grain. Against all odds, the baby Sara survived. In contrast to my father, my mother grew up in a home that secretly but steadfastly maintained its Mennonite faith despite the constant pressure of the communist state. Sara was eight when collectiviza-tion came to Osterwick. She remembered how hard it was for her father to give up everything he had worked for. In contrast to my father's stories, my mother dwelt more on how she felt. She recalled, for instance, the intense tension that came with the communist-inspired "Pioneer" movement for younger children:

> It was difficult. In school, you were told that you had to become a "Pioneer," the others were all going to be "Pioneers." Our parents said that this was not according to the teachings of the Bible and that we shouldn't do it: "We believe, and we pray, but don't say this, don't tell them this." It was—it was so [hard] not being able to say that your parents didn't let you. Well, I didn't want to either, but always putting yourself in that position: "I don't want to." At home, every day they said, "Don't become a Pioneer"; in school, "Yes, be-come a Pioneer!"[1]

Sara was called into the office and promised that she would get to wear new clothes if she joined the Pioneers and wear the characteristic red scarf, but the influence of her family kept her from joining.

Her aunt Greta, who lived with them, was a powerful influence on young Sara. Greta continued to read Bible stories to her and her brother Jacob even though it was expressly forbidden by the state. My mother attributed her be-ing able to remain true to the faith to her aunt. As she told the story, "It had a big influence on you if, day after day, they try to prove to you [that there is no God], not only tell you, but prove it to you. Then I would go home, and a big dog would come, and I would pray, or the boys in school would want to hit me, and then they would let me go, and I would think, 'Oh, yes, there is a God.'"[2]

Although Sara had been born during a famine, the 1933 Ukrainian famine was seared into her memory. She was twelve, and there was no food. The family sat around the kitchen table sorting through spilled and cracked grain that had been saved for the pigeons in order to find a few kernels of grain or beans to make soup. Even those few kernels were taken away when the authorities swept the attic of the barn. Sara was sick. There was hardly any food, and she seemingly could not eat what little there was. In school, the children were given a kind of porridge soup, but when she caught a whiff of it she became nauseous and had to leave the room to avoid retching. At home, she could not eat, and all day she sat "hunched up somewhere in a corner, the entire summer." As soon as she awoke in the morning, she sat down in the corner with her knees pulled up against her stomach; it was the only way she felt comfortable. She salivated constantly, "pails full, wherever I sat, such a pool, just saliva."[3]

Sara survived the famine, which abated in 1934. Gradually the kolkhoz began to take hold; the state relented somewhat in its grain procurements, and the Mennonite farmers resigned themselves to making the farm work. Sara began to work on the collective farm even before she finished school, and in 1935 or 1936 she became a full-time collective farm worker. About the same time, her half-sister Tina married Julius Vogt, and her leaving the household to establish a separate household meant one kolkhoz worker's earnings were lost to the family. Sara was working full time by then, and 1936 proved to be the best year ever; the amount per trudanye paid out to the workers never reached the same level again. There were further disruptions during the purges of the 1930s, and, while they affected some in the village who had been considered kulaks, the Letkeman family survived the late 1930s relatively unscathed. Sara's mother's family, the Woelkes, had been wealthy, and many relatives on that side of the family suffered exile.

On the eve of the Second World War, Sara was an eighteen-year-old collective farm worker. The beginning of the war in September 1939 was not really that noticeable in the collective farm along the Dnieper River. The secret Ribbentrop–Molotov Pact, which pledged non-aggression between Stalin and Hitler, meant that the war going on in Europe was not really noted by Sara. Her mother, however, was very interested in politics and a regular reader of the German newspaper *Das Neue Dorf.* As my mother said, she could read not only what was printed on the page but also what was not said between the lines of this communist newspaper. A few of their Russian neighbours were drafted into the army to serve in the Finnish Winter War in 1939–40, but no one from their village was called up. The rhythms of the collective farm remained, and summers meant long days and weeks without

Sara Letkeman together with fellow collective farm workers in Osterwick on a Sunday in 1939. She is the second from the right in the second row.

a day of rest. That was also the case in the summer of 1941, when Sara and other collective farm workers had worked for weeks without a break. Sunday, 22 June, was the first day in a long time they had a break. It was not really a day of rest since there were laundry and other chores to be done. Sometime during the day, Sara's brother Jacob came to tell them that Germany had attacked the Soviet Union. The whole village was excited, and everyone worried about the implications of being a German-speaking minority in a country that had now been attacked by Germany.

Things changed immediately. Armed guards were posted throughout the village, and that night when the young people assembled on the village street they were sent home. No lights were permitted. "You had to grope around in the dark for everything." Sara remained in Osterwick only a few more days before she was sent south toward the Crimea to cook for a construction crew building a highway. The kolkhoz had to supply a crew of four men and twelve women for this construction effort. Her story became quite cryptic when she talked about this experience. In the beginning, the group stayed with a Russian family who, she recalled, had been very nice to them. It seems their accommodations changed later, and the village filled up with Russian men, soldiers, and support personnel for the military buildup. Without explaining, my mother said, "then at night they would come around—I was fortunate." Apparently drunken men would come to get her to cook for them in the middle of the night, and she felt vulnerable and threatened. After feeding them, Sara and a friend slept in the hallway in front of the bedroom door behind which a group of married men slept. They felt safer there. Later they got away and slept in a barn; she thought they had "been lucky" to "get away from there." They did not sleep that night for fear of being found. Later in the story, she referred to those who "came for the girls that night" as officers. In contrast, the Red Army soldiers who came back from the front soon after were nice to them and told them stories about the horror of the initial attack by the Germans.[4]

Sara had a boyfriend before the German attack who had been drafted into the Red Army. Even in the confusion of the war, she received a letter that arrived after she left Osterwick but was delivered to her by someone from there. The letter had obviously been written before the attack, and her boyfriend expressed confusion about what was going on. He had been released from the army, and the insignia had been removed from his cap. He could not tell her where he was. This troubling letter and the realization that the war was going badly for the Soviet Union convinced Sara and other girls that they needed to return to Osterwick. They tried to convince their supervisor, a Mr. Siemens, to allow them to return with a wagon that had come from Osterwick with supplies, but he refused. They decided to go anyway and left on foot.

The girls walked all day to get to Kichkas, where miraculously they were able to buy train tickets to Zaporozhye. At the train station, fear again gripped Sara as everywhere she looked there were unaccompanied men. On the train, a young man opened the door to ask if there was anyone on the train from Schoenberg, a village next to Osterwick. He was a former classmate, and with tears streaming down his face he asked them to greet his parents, for he did not know if he would ever see them again. All he knew was that he was being sent away. The already stressful train ride became worse when the doors to their car were thrown open and they were accused of being German spies. After some time, they convinced the police they were not German spies, but their problems soon became more serious. When the train got to Zaporozhye, the tracks across the Dnieper River and the dam had already been bombed. When they reached the city, they really became aware that they were getting closer to the front.

My mother's memory was unclear about details of these events. The stress, constant fear, and chaos that accompanied the journey contributed to her confusion. The Mennonite village of Einlage, renamed Kichkas in 1941, was on the right bank of the Dnieper, the same side as Osterwick. That seems to indicate that the girls were north of Osterwick rather than in the Crimea and would have had to cross the Dnieper to get as close to Osterwick by train as possible. Her memory seemed to fail my mother when she told these stories, which she attributed to confusion and stress. As she put it, "I don't think I was quite normal anymore."[5] Bombing of the bridges over the Dnieper meant that they could not cross the river by train, but it seems that planks had been laid across the damaged sections of the bridge so that a horse-drawn vehicle could still cross. It was twilight before they found someone in the sea of men who would take them across the river. They got home when it was already dark. It was her birthday, 13 August, and after an initial scare when she found the house empty, Sara found the rest of the family intact. She reported to the kolkhoz headquarters the next day to explain their return and found that all the girls had found their way back, but Siemens, the supervisor, and the other men had not returned. The village was in turmoil, and secretly plans were being made to escape to the German lines, which everyone thought must be nearby.

For Sara's family, the option of escaping to the German lines was unrealistic. Her father was seventy years old, had poor eyesight, and walked with a cane. Her brother Jacob, sixteen, had been ordered to hitch up a wagon to transport Jews across the Dnieper. On 10 August, her half-sister Tina's husband had been sent across the river with animals and farm equipment.[6] Sara's parents had decided not to let Jacob go and hid him instead. While Sara was away, they had dug a hole in the small orchard in their yard and covered it with planks and sod to make a small shelter. Jacob spent the day in this shelter. The night of 16 August and all the next day the family stayed in the shelter because of the constant shelling and gunfire. The makeshift bunker kept getting smaller as walls caved in from the vibrations of explosions. From time to time, they heard someone banging on the doors of their house, and it was hard to keep Tina's young children from crying and giving away their hiding place. Finally toward evening it got quieter, and Sara left the bunker to go to the neighbour's house. She knocked on the door, only to be greeted by three Red Army soldiers, who immediately yelled *"Stoi!"* when she turned to run. In spite of their command to stop or be shot, Sara ran through the bushes, the long grass, and the creek to arrive back in the shelter, shaking but unharmed. The family spent that night in their house in an otherwise empty village—everyone had left. Sara's mother decided they could still be sent to the east, away from the advancing Germans, and began baking in preparation. My mother could not recall if she completed baking, but she had mixed the dough. At two or three in the morning, the village came alive with retreating Red Army military vehicles. At daybreak, the constant noise of vehicles ended, and "it was quiet. Over here you could hear a sheep bleating, there you could hear a cow bellowing, here a dog would bark; it echoed everywhere."[7]

At nine o'clock in the morning on 18 August, a cloud of dust marked the advance of the German Army. After briefly hiding in a granary on their yard, Sara's family came out to greet the black-uniformed soldiers of the panzer army that had advanced to the Dnieper River at Zaporozhye. Gradually over the next hours and days, people returned to the village. Some had hidden in cornfields while on their way east to cross the Dnieper; others had been overtaken trying to escape and returned to their homes under German occupation.[8]

For my mother, the story was one of liberation. It was the German Army that freed them from Stalin's clutches, and she was forever grateful in spite of the story that emerged about Nazi atrocities. Her memories of the Nazi liberation were what Steve Stern terms "memory as salvation," a way of remembering that acknowledges evil done but frames it as necessary because it offered salvation to the person remembering.[9] In contrast to my father, for my mother the memories of becoming German in the Nazi context were used to tell stories in ways that reflected her desire to view the escape from Stalinism as a positive and justifiable experience rather than as a product of a regime guilty of atrocities.

Life under German occupation was refreshing at first. The Sunday after the front passed over them and they were under German occupation, some villagers met for a church service at the Anton Krahn house, the first time in many years that the community had worshipped together. It was important to my mother to point out in her story that the sermon was offered by a passing German soldier who happened to be a Lutheran pastor.[10] The people attending "had not been able to sing, they had only cried." Over the next few weeks, worship services were established on a regular basis in the schoolhouse, and Mennonite cultural life resumed, a relief from the oppressive communist ideology that had overshadowed everything. The first Christmas under German occupation was memorable; my mother told the story while sobbing intermittently: "It was very nice; it was the first Christmas after so many years. In the clubhouse, the building that had been the club during Soviet times, there we had our Christmas program. The youth brought baked goods; we made little bags.... There were a lot of girls, and the boys carried the bags away when they were filled. We filled the bags there and had a program, just like we do here except—you know, they were so emotional."[11]

The resumption of religious observance also meant that baptisms could again become part of the life cycle of the Mennonite people of Osterwick. On 24 May 1942, Gerhard Dueck baptized Sara in their church.[12] But one dark cloud hung over the Letkeman family. Julius Vogt, husband of Tina, had been sent east and not returned. The war front now separated Tina from him, and she had effectively become a widow, so the relief they all felt was tempered by the sadness of separation. It also meant Tina was again part of the Letkeman household, and by now she had two children: Erwin, two-and-a-half years old, and Marie, just five months old.

Although some collective farms in occupied Ukraine reverted to private ownership, in Osterwick too many men were missing, so the German occupation government decided to keep the kolkhoz intact. In the first few days after the front passed, the remaining horses, livestock, and equipment were collected, and the harvest resumed. The grain was now destined for the German war effort, but Mennonites had become prized members of the master race and got more per trudanye than they had before and more than their Slavic counterparts would get during the German occupation.

Living under German occupation was not without tension, and soon Sara became aware of moral dilemmas that came with the Mennonites' new status as Germans. In one case, a Mennonite woman who had married a Ukrainian refused to take him back as her husband even though the Germans released him from a POW camp because he had a German wife. One Mennonite woman had married a Jew, who then disappeared and was likely shot, but the woman and her children were spared. A Ukrainian woman who was married to a Jew gave her children into the care of her sister and died with her husband.

There were also moral dilemmas for Sara. She was now the primary breadwinner for her family, and if she took a job working for the German occupation government she got paid in currency rather than an amount of grain or produce per trudanye in the kolkhoz. That was worth a lot. Her first job was cooking for the supply troops who stayed in the area for a number of months. After they left, she was the cook for the night watchmen who worked for the German occupation. They were mostly Ukrainians who had declared themselves willing to help the Germans, but their supervisors were Mennonite men whom Sara knew. In 1942, these watchmen were ordered to round up the Jews in the area and take them to some undisclosed destination and shoot them. As my mother recalled, "it was terrible when they came home, they felt terribly badly about what they had to do." Cooking for the occupation police proved to be too much emotional strain for Sara, and she quit. She witnessed the police arresting and imprisoning people who came from cities nearer to the front to gather food because it was in such short supply. "It bothered me terribly when they imprisoned those poor people." She also felt increasingly at risk working alone with a group of policemen, who were steadily becoming "brasher."[13]

The new identity that Sara and other Mennonites had acquired of being favoured as ethnic Germans in an occupied Ukraine was made most clear to her when she went to pick up her first paycheque after working for the German occupation government. When she gave her name as Sara, the clerk said they had no Sara Letkeman on the payroll, but they did have a Frieda Letkeman. When she investigated, it turned out the soldiers had renamed her Frieda because it was unacceptable for someone with a Jewish name like Sara to be in the employ of the Germans. In defiance of being named by some soldiers, she formally chose her own German name, Margarethe.

The German Army began to flounder in the harsh Russian winters, and when it failed to capture Stalingrad in the winter of 1942–43 its fate was sealed. By the spring of 1943, the glow of the artillery shells exploding on the front could be seen on clear evenings, and then the rumble of cannons could be heard in Osterwick on quiet nights. Soviet airplanes began bombing threshing floors, and a sad sight replaced my mother's memory of the dashing German soldiers who had come through Osterwick in the summer of 1941. "It looked sad the way they came back. They had Russian girls all over their vehicles, everywhere there were Russian girls whom they were bringing along—it looked very bad when they came back."[14] Margarethe and the other Mennonites of Osterwick began to worry. There was talk of being evacuated, assurances that the Germans would not abandon them, but when would that happen?

The time came. On 18 and 19 October 1943, the villagers of Osterwick were loaded onto army trucks and taken to Kantserovka (Rosenthal), the nearest train station, and loaded onto trains headed for the Warthegau, the area of Poland annexed by Germany and already home to many resettled Baltic and Polish Germans. Margarethe's family left on 19 October.[15] It was a rainy evening, and to avoid the Soviet bombers the train was scheduled to leave at night. They travelled through the night, stopping frequently due to damaged tracks. The train took them to Litzmannstadt, where their first assignment was to be deloused. They were taken in buses to the Kitler factory, where their clothes were baked in ovens and they had an insecticide-laced shower. After three or four days in Litzmannstadt, Margarethe and her family were moved to Beneschau, where they lived in a large castle-like building with many other resettled ethnic Germans. Christmas 1943 was celebrated there, and in my mother's memory it was wonderful to return to earlier traditions. Margarethe worked in the kitchen, while other ethnic Germans worked in a tobacco factory. Just after Christmas, she married Peter Vogt.

Her first boyfriend's letter, which she received just before the German occupation, had acknowledged that they might never see each other again and released her from their relationship. Peter Vogt, a cousin of Tina's husband Julius Vogt, had already been interested in Margarethe during the German occupation period. He had been drafted into the German Army or one of its ancillary organizations and come back to Osterwick after being wounded. He had been hit in the leg by shrapnel in an engagement in which three or four other young Osterwick men had been killed.[16] Margarethe had always rejected his advances because of her sense of obligation to her aging parents. She could not see herself marrying when it was unclear how her parents would be cared for. That sensibility was somewhat resolved by the formal admission to German citizenship, which occurred shortly after they arrived in the Warthegau. Her parents received an old age pension from the German government, and the war brought other changes in attitude. As she noted, "In situations like that, the person just thinks about today and tomorrow, you don't think any further. If today you are healthy and have enough to eat, what will be tomorrow, you don't know. If you are alive today, if you die tomorrow, it doesn't matter. You actually have no worries, what you will eat, what you will wear; the worries are actually taken away from you. If you are living, you don't know anything, you are just alive; about tomorrow, you know nothing; it gives you an entirely different feeling."[17] Peter and Margarethe had been married for about two months when Peter was drafted into the German Army. In spring 1944, she received her German citizenship.[18] Although she had no particular objection to being a German citizen, the process was degrading. Like Johann a year earlier, she had to appear naked in front of a panel of seven "doctors" for a medical examination that was really a racial examination.

In late summer 1944, Margarethe and her family were moved to Ratibor in Upper Silesia. They lived in a camp with 350 or so other resettled Mennonites. Margarethe was pregnant with her first child, so she did not go to work but took care of Tina's two children and their elderly parents. The front kept getting nearer, and soon Soviet air raids were a constant and worrisome danger. Margarethe gave birth to her first child at night in the camp's small sickroom. While she was in labour, there was an air raid, and the midwife was reluctant to come. Margarethe suffered considerable tearing during the birth and in the confusion did not receive the necessary stitches and became infected. The baby was a healthy girl whom she named Katharina but who was always called Katie. Margarethe was unable to nurse the baby; her breasts became swollen and infected, and she had to go to the hospital. During her hospital stay, constant air raids sent patients to the hospital's air raid shelter to escape the bombing. In the shelter, people screamed when bombs exploded nearby, and the whole bunker shook from the concussions of the explosions. After the air raids, the wounded were brought into the hospital, often completely blackened by fire and smoke. The doctors then went to work, and people in the hospital claimed there were literally piles of limbs in the operating room that had been amputated from victims. When the doctors made their rounds, they looked like they had worked in a slaughterhouse.

When Margarethe was released from the hospital, she walked back to the camp but was unable to recognize Ratibor. Everywhere there were signs warning pedestrians not to walk in certain places because of unexploded shells. Houses were piles of rubble. She had to ask passersby which street she was on so she could navigate her way back home, where she feared the worst. Fortunately all were safe. Soon, however, even her brother Jacob, who had been spared the draft because of his extreme short-sightedness, was also called up. Margarethe and Tina went to see him when he had completed some basic training and was being sent to the front. A few letters arrived from her husband Peter, who urgently told her to leave everything and save herself and the baby. His plea weighed heavily on her in the weeks to come.

On 12 January 1945, the Red Army launched a massive attack to cross the Vistula River, and on 25 January German military vehicles with loudspeakers were on the streets of Ratibor telling everyone to flee for their lives.[19] Margarethe and her family were a sorry lot. Her parents were in their seventies; her younger brother and husband were away, their fate unknown; her half-sister Tina had two small children and a husband left behind somewhere in the east; and Margarethe had an infant a few months old. They joined hundreds of other refugees in horse-drawn wagons in a desperate flight over the Sudeten Mountains into Czechoslovakia in exceptionally cold weather. On the way to Troppau (Opava), the refugee caravan was strafed by Soviet fighter–bombers, and the refugees were forced to abandon their wagons for the ditches. Mothers had wrapped their children tightly to ward against the cold and in the panic clasped them even more tightly. Many children suffocated. When they reached Troppau, Margarethe went to the train station to see the little blue bodies piled up on the platform. Her own daughter had survived, for which she was relieved and immensely grateful because she could not imagine having to tell Peter that she had suffocated their daughter. In Troppau, Margarethe and her family were loaded onto trains and travelled to Oderburg, where they remained for a day or two. In my mother's memory, the events of these days were disjointed, and it was apparent that Margarethe had been mentally and physically at her limit.

In Oderburg, the elderly were taken away, and Margarethe and her half-sister were separated from their parents and her uncle Peter, who was travelling with them. In my mother's memory, this separation came in the context of a rumour that the old were to be euthanized. All they could do was pray: "we prayed so hard, where could our father have stayed?" There were so many people, and all they could hope for was that their elderly family members would catch a glimpse of the red hat that Margarethe always wore. It was mass confusion: "they came and called the men, all old people, and we didn't know what was going on." Some people claimed the old men had all been loaded into vehicles and taken away. Toward morning, they all came back and told stories of having been shuffled between vehicles and then suddenly dropped off at the train station again. After two days of tension and confusion in Oderburg, the family members were reunited and loaded onto a train to continue their journey to the west, away from the advancing Red Army.[20]

Margarethe deteriorated to the point that her fellow refugees thought she was close to death, and they worried they would end up burying her beside the road. Understandably there is considerable interference in the memories of my mother about the exact sequence of events during these difficult days. Her memories do not place importance on where she was on which day. She remembers much more clearly the small acts of kindness shown to her by people on the refugee flight: the woman in the train station who invited her inside and gave her milk for the baby and a change of clothes after the harrowing flight to Troppau, the transport leader who always came to check on how she was doing, the unidentified soldier who gave up his lice-infested straw mattress so she could lie down and rest.

The train eventually passed through Dresden, and in my mother's memory they stopped at Dresden just a few days after it was firebombed by Allied bombers on 13 and 14 February, though accounts by other travelling companions suggest they had come through Dresden a week or more earlier.[21] Margarethe and her extended family were unloaded at Wernigerode in central Germany and transferred to a camp with no food, no bedding, and a director who was rude, especially to women and children. They became beggars and were grateful when people were not rude to them, even if they did not give them anything. There was no sleep to be had with nightly bombing and constantly hungry children. When air raid sirens screamed in the night, it meant going down to the basement among the water pipes, where they were sure to drown if the exploding bombs did not kill them.

Then suddenly they had to move. In their minds, there was no purpose to moving. If they were all to die anyway, the camp near Wernigerode was as good as anywhere. But they moved nevertheless. The move was only a short distance to the village of Lautenthal, some sixteen kilometres from Wernigerode. The move was fortuitous for them. A few weeks later the borders were drawn for what would become the east zone under the control of Stalin and the western zones under the control of the Allies. Wernigerode would be in the Russian zone, while Lautenthal would be in the British zone.

The war ended for Margarethe and her family on the morning of 11 April, the same day as her future husband Johann was captured near Unna. Early that morning when the sun was just up the Americans came, "every four metres a soldier," with their rifles at the ready. By this time, they had heard such horror stories of what would happen when the Americans came that they could only conclude their final hours had arrived.[22]

In the weeks after the end of the war, an order came for their entire group to be ready to move again. They were loaded onto military trucks and taken to the Goslar train station to be sent back to the Soviet Union. The prospect of going back held some appeal. For Margarethe's sister Tina, it meant possibly being reunited with her husband; for her parents, it offered the hope of seeing her brother Jacob. But it also meant returning to the world of Stalin and the oppression that came with it. In the Goslar train station, they were given K-rations, the train was decorated with boughs of evergreen tree branches, and the hammer and sickle appeared everywhere. The group of women, old people, and children decided they were not going to the Soviet Union. In spite of the prods from the rifle butts of the Red Army soldiers and the rows of *ostarbeiter* filing by them heading for the train, four abreast and singing Ukrainian folk songs, they refused to board the train. A British commander arrived and through an interpreter tried to convince them to go to their homeland rather than starve in a devastated Germany. They remained unconvinced and told him that, "if Germany was to starve, we were going to starve with her, we were not going back to Russia." In a remarkable display of passive resistance, they told the officer it made no difference to them where they died and did not need to travel a long way to die in the end anyway. The officer relented and advised them a truck would come in the evening to take them somewhere. They did not know where or what would await them.[23]

The truck that came took them to Rammelsberg, an abandoned silver mine in the Harz Mountains just outside Goslar. It had been a camp for the *ostarbeiter*, and there they were unloaded to fend for themselves. They were literally starving, relegated to eating the crusts that Uncle Peter found in the garbage and using the discarded coffee grounds to make coffee. Contact with a former soldier who had been in Chortitza during the war put them in touch with an estate farm called Ohlehof, where they were able to find work. A Dr. Lampe managed the estate. He needed workers since the estate's entire Eastern European forced labour force had gone home. At first, the estate came to pick them up each day with a tractor and wagon, but eventually they moved into a chicken barn on the estate itself. Margarethe was terribly weak and could hardly manage the work. Her first job was spreading manure, but she was so weak she could hardly lift a fork full of manure. After a short time, she was soaked in sweat, and her arms started to swell.

Margarethe was fortunate to be taken aside to work in the supervisor's home, where special treatment and additional food allowed her to gradually regain her strength. But her daughter Katie never recovered from the refugee flight. Although she had survived the harrowing flight over the Sudeten Mountains when so many other children suffocated, she was never healthy again and now had contracted tuberculosis. While they were at Ohlehof, she was placed in a sanatorium, but the doctors offered little hope. Margarethe took three months off work to care for Katie, but she died in her arms in 1947. Katie was buried in the small cemetery on the estate. She was just over two years old.

The group of refugees in the chicken barns in Ohlehof lived in constant fear that Stalin would not stop at the line just east of where they were and that they would again fall into Soviet hands. Upon reflection, my mother recalled that it must have seemed she had lost her mind entirely even though the war was over. Ever since they had left Ratibor, she had received no news of her husband Peter, and whenever she could she spent hours at the Goslar train station watching the trains with POWs on board arrive, hoping he might magically come walking off the train. It did not happen. Margarethe and her parents had the same hope for Jacob, but he also never appeared. For her half-sister Tina, there was no such hope. She knew her husband Julius had stayed behind in the Soviet Union.

Eventually C.F. Klassen, the untiring MCC refugee worker from Canada, visited the small group of refugees on the Ohlehof estate. My mother recalled how the news spread that a Canadian was coming to visit. She and her family had the largest accommodations of the Mennonite group that worked at Ohlehof, so the entire group met with Klassen in their home. It was a memorable evening. Klassen seemed to know everyone's relatives in Canada. The group stayed up until the early hours of the next day questioning Klassen about family and friends in Canada. The visit signalled the beginning of the attempt to emigrate to Canada.

Canada's requirements were stringent, and the prospects for her aging parents to gain admission were slim. Margarethe was eligible for emigration to Canada right away. The problems getting admission to Canada for their parents drove Tina to opt for the whole family to move to Paraguay. She had already sacrificed purchasing bread to buy saws, axes, and wire mesh for the windows of their eventual house in Paraguay. Margarethe, generally the less aggressive of the two, had gone along with the idea initially but finally could not envision the "ragtag" family making it on the frontier in the Gran Chaco of Paraguay. They had already received a letter with the date of their departure when Margarethe changed her mind. She mustered her resolve while Tina was already packing. She told Tina she was not going to Paraguay and left the room. When she returned later that night after it was dark, Tina got out of bed and confronted her about the alternative, which in her mind meant falling into the hands of the Soviets. Margarethe remained steadfast and reminded her half-sister that she would not be the one to do all the work in Paraguay because of her young children. Even in Ohlehof, only Margarethe was able to work to support the entire family.

But emigrating to Canada was not working out because of the age and health of her parents. Margarethe could emigrate whenever she wanted, but she refused to leave her parents behind. Tina found a sponsor in Canada and left Germany in October 1949 with her two children, Erwin and Marie, to settle in Drake, Saskatchewan.[24] When Margarethe met Johann Werner in the Gronau camp, she was still trying to find a way to emigrate to Canada with her parents.

Like those of Johann, Margarethe's memories were also difficult to frame into stories in the context of a postwar Mennonite family in small-town Manitoba. Stories about her first marriage and the daughter who had died were not told. But her sharp sense of "telling the truth" also meant that Margarethe could not keep these stories entirely secret. Inevitably in various contexts and at different times, she allowed fragments of the story to become known. In contrast to Johann's stories, Margarethe always framed hers from the point of view of preservation of the faith she had learned from her aunt and faith on a broader level as part of the Mennonite church. Stalin's Soviet Union could then be framed as purely evil because of its overt challenge to Mennonite faith. Hitler's Germany, on the other hand, could be embraced because it maintained the language of supporting Christian faith as part of German culture even as it worked to undermine that faith by substituting Nazi ideology.

The Immigrants

THE COUPLE WHO STOOD BEFORE THE MINISTER Gerhard Fast on that September afternoon in 1951 to be married had biographies spoiled during the war years. It is not entirely clear how much they knew about each other's respective history, but it is apparent that Margarethe had been more forthcoming in narrating her story than Johann had been in his. Nevertheless, they apparently agreed that their pasts were best left behind them, and it was understood that what had happened before was not to be raised in their relationship. Margarethe had withdrawn her application to emigrate when her parents had been turned down by Canadian authorities, and her anticipated marriage to Johann complicated her desire to emigrate together with her elderly parents if they should eventually be admitted. He had put the idea of emigration behind him and resigned himself to making a place for himself in a Germany that was quickly rebuilding after the war. Johann and Margarethe applied for a house to be built by the MCC's PAX program, and, for her at least, there was a reluctant resignation that they might not be joining her parents even if they were able to emigrate to Canada. Her half-sister Tina, meanwhile, continued to search for a way for that to happen from her new home in Drake, Saskatchewan.

Just days before Tina and her children emigrated to Canada on 16 October 1949, the Canadian government again rejected Margarethe's parents' admission into Canada for medical reasons. A summary of their situation in a file of MCC's "hard core" cases notes only that they were apparently rejected

Johann and Margarethe on their wedding day, 24 September 1951.

because of "old age and physical decrepancies [sic]."[1] The disappointing letter from the Canadian Government Immigration Mission stated simply that their "application for admission to Canada... has not been approved."[2] With their daughter Tina now in Canada, there was the possibility that she could sponsor the elderly couple, but they were becoming weary of all the problems. Margarethe would not consider a suggestion that a permanent home for her parents could be a seniors' home in Germany.

In August 1951, just before Johann and Margarethe got married, news came that her parents were eligible to appear for processing for Canadian immigration based on the strength of the sponsorship of their daughter Tina and another relative in Drake. In October, they went to Gronau for processing, and on 23 February 1952 the long-awaited visas arrived. The elderly couple, now sixty-eight and eighty-one years old, left Bremerhaven on the ship the *Beaverbrae* on 12 April to join their daughter in Drake.[3] Margarethe was now faced with being separated from them because of Johann. Her letters to the MCC convey the urgency of the need to resolve her own emigration status. She advised the MCC that, "if my parents should make it over, then I would like to emigrate. But I would first like to marry Hans Werner, whom you also have in your files."[4] The process of trying to emigrate began in earnest again for Johann.

Although the reason for his early rejection by Canadian authorities because he had become a German citizen in 1942 was no longer an impediment, Johann continued to be turned back. The accusation that he had been in the SS now loomed large in his file and had to be overcome. On 7 April 1952, C.F. Klassen wrote to P.W. Bird, chief of the Canadian Immigration Mission in Karlsruhe, about the SS cases that had not been approved for emigration. Johann and Margarethe Werner were included on the list of difficult cases to be discussed.[5] On 30 April, the MCC chartered a bus to transport a group of SS cases to Hanover. The Werners were in the group that appeared before the commission that day. They had yet another medical examination, were subjected to what was termed Stage B security screening, and were "also seen by the Labour Man," as the MCC secretary put it. Johann did not get permission to emigrate but was "labelled 'pending' for Stage 'B.'" In short, he had been deferred again, but rather than the problem of his naturalization it was only because of suspicions that he had been an early SS member.[6]

Waiting is a mark of being a refugee, and Johann and Margarethe now waited again. Meanwhile, a letter from Margarethe to the MCC requesting a baby parcel betrayed another new beginning. They were expecting their first child. Then, without warning on 20 June 1952, urgent telegrams arrived from the MCC notifying them that they had been granted entry into Canada. Margarethe responded to the news with relief but worried because they were "expecting their baby in the middle of October," and it certainly would have been more suitable if the news had come earlier so they could make the journey in June.[7] The various MCC offices that had to arrange transportation sprang into action to make it possible for the couple to get to Canada before the ship's policies on the transport of pregnant passengers would prevent their sailing until after the baby was born. As MCC Secretary Anne Giesbrecht explained to J.J. Thiessen, head of the Canadian Mennonite Board of Colonization, "we had to do everything possible to get ship passage for them because of Mrs. Werner's pregnancy, and by the time of the next sailing it would have been too late and she would have had to wait until the baby was born."[8] The last day of work for Johann was 24 June, and four days later he and Margarethe boarded the *Beaverbrae* for the trip across the ocean to Canada.[9]

The stories of their trip to Canada and the early days of adjusting to a new country needed to be a collaboration of their memories of these shared experiences and had to resolve each of their memories to produce a common narrative. Johann now deferred to Margarethe for many of the stories of their shared experiences. The ocean passage was difficult for a woman who was six months pregnant, but Margarethe proudly noted it had not been as difficult for her as it had been for Johann. She was berthed midship and did not experience as much of the heaving and did not get sick. Johann, however, got terribly seasick. He was in the bow and complained bitterly that where he was they went up and down a lot more than in the middle of the ship. Once when he went outside onto the deck for fresh air someone on the deck above was hanging over the rail and vomiting. It was very unpleasant, and years later when the children burped or vomited he had to leave the room immediately. There were more pleasant memories of the passage. Johann and Margarethe remembered seeing icebergs when they neared Newfoundland. They were dismayed, however, at the long sail up the St. Lawrence with only the odd village church steeple to be seen. They finally disembarked in Quebec on 9 July 1952.[10]

Schiff „Beaverbrae" bei der Ausfahrt von Bremen nach Canada

The CP ship, Beaverbrae, part of reparations after the war, became the ship for emigrants on their way to Canada in the postwar years. Johann and Margarethe Werner left Bremen on the Beaverbrae on 28 June 1952 and arrived at Quebec City on 9 July 1952.

The sailing of the *Beaverbrae* from Bremen triggered the assembly of two trains of colonist cars at Quebec, timed to coincide with the ship's arrival, with one destined for Montreal and Toronto and one for Winnipeg and points west.[11] My parents recalled the experience of the train leaving southern Ontario, and after a few hours the endless rocks, forests, and lakes were all they could see from the train's windows. A particularly lively German woman who was a war bride on her way to join her husband and his family in northern Ontario had been the "life of the party" in the early stages. When the train travelled for hours through the Canadian Shield without any evidence of human settlement, she became progressively quieter. Johann and Margarethe vividly recalled the scene of the small family assembled on the platform at a remote town in northwest Ontario that was her new home. The whole car strained to get a glimpse of this new beginning, but it was hard for anyone to imagine the adjustments she faced.

Along the unending railway tracks, the German-speaking immigrants were thrilled at the signs announcing what they thought were German city names, only to realize that in Canada Regina was pronounced very differently than the sound that rolled off their German tongues. Margarethe and Johann were headed for Swift Current, where a relative of Margarethe's mother's first husband had sponsored them under the Farm Worker Scheme. Their Canadian sponsor, Peter Dyck, picked them up at the Swift Current station to begin their life on a Saskatchewan farm.

An almost morbid irony infused the story of my father's first days in Canada. The Dyck farm was small, and a few days after they arrived a granary was to be moved on the farmyard. Johann was given the task of standing by with a rifle as the granary began to move to shoot the skunks that would emerge due to the disturbance. It was thought that, since he had been a soldier, he would naturally be able to shoot better than the other farmers, whose conscientious objector status had spared them military training. Shooting skunks on a Canadian Mennonite farm village was a long way from the daily horrors of war. Although it was brief, the interaction with the Dyck family, who belonged to a more conservative Mennonite group, was an eye-opener for the new arrivals. In contrast to their experiences, the life of the conservative Mennonite family on the sparsely populated prairie seemed narrow and limited. Johann and Margarethe did not stay in Swift Current long. The Dyck farm was too small to provide steady work for Johann, and the rest of her family, including her parents, lived in Drake, a considerable distance northeast of Swift Current. During the month Johann and Margarethe were in Swift Current, he repaired the Dycks' farm equipment for the upcoming harvest. Her half-sister Tina tried to find Johann a job in Drake and was successful for the fall harvest.

Sandy Blair, Johann's new employer in Drake, operated a large farm, and his harvesting equipment included a number of combines and trucks. Johann had no time to settle into their new home but went directly from the car that had brought him and a pregnant Margarethe to Drake to the combine on the Blair farm. One hot harvest day Dale, the youngest of Blair's sons, about twelve years old and hardly tall enough to see over the steering wheel, was driving a grain truck. When the truck drove by his combine, Johann glimpsed a fire under it. He immediately began cleaning up the swaths near the fire to prevent it from spreading. The other combines also joined the effort and, with the rest of the crew, were able to extinguish the fire before it consumed the entire field. Although grateful for their quick action, Blair accused the combine operators of being careless by tossing their still lit cigarette butts onto the desiccated grain field. Johann had seen Dale drive across a swath and suspected that straw had been forced too close to the exhaust system, where it had begun to smoulder and eventually set the field on fire. Blair did not speak German, and Johann spoke no English. The only way he could finally convey to Blair what had happened was by taking him by the hand to the truck to see for himself the still smouldering straw underneath it.

These stories of finding his way in a strange land, and in somewhat embarrassing circumstances, were part of my father's repertoire. When told many years later, they were conveyed nostalgically and with a certain fondness for the challenges of his early days in Canada. Not many of his stories portrayed the depths of pain and worry associated with starting over in a strange land. Those stories were left to my mother to tell.

The arrangement with Sandy Blair was that he would provide them with a house in exchange for their providing room and board for another two workers and for Margarethe to cook meals for the harvest crews. That was hard work since she was eight months pregnant. The house was about nine miles from Drake on the open prairie. When Blair was asked about allowing her parents to move in with them, his answer was no, he was not operating an old folks' home.

There were immediate financial pressures. The Canadian Mennonite Board of Colonization had financed the trip to Canada, and the debt had to be repaid. An April 1953 letter from the board listed Johann and Margarethe's payments of over $400. The letter was addressed to John Werner. Sometime after he arrived in Canada, Johann had become John, while Margarethe had become Margaret. Along with financial pressures came joys but also grief and loss. On 5 October 1952, the couple's first child was born in the Lanigan hospital. I was named Hans Peter, after my father and likely after Margaret's first husband. Her half-sister, together with her children and parents, lived in Drake in a house owned by the church. Tina had a part-time job cleaning the church, for which she was paid forty dollars a month and free use of the house.[12] But early in 1953 she became ill with cancer and died on 23 March. Her children, Erwin and Marie, fourteen and eleven, became orphans. Tina's death and the birth of a baby meant that the number of dependants who looked to John and Margaret for their livelihoods had jumped from two in Germany to five within the first few months of their arrival in Canada.[13]

Although Margaret's aged parents did not have to move out of the house immediately, the question of where they and the two children would stay and how they would live became more pressing. John had fulfilled his promised year of farm work, and the decision was made to quit work at the Blair farm to take up a job as an auto mechanic in Drake. That would allow them to move into town and afforded them the opportunity of having the grandparents live with them. It also soon became clear that, though the two orphan children had relatives in Drake, they were looking to John and Margaret to take care of them.

In November 1953, John started work at a small garage in Drake at a salary of $250 a month.[14] The move was a disaster. The owner of the garage had his own problems, and John had to beg to get even ten dollars of the wages he had earned. By February 1954, he could go on no longer and negotiated for a pickup truck as part payment of the wages owed to him. He borrowed money from Margaret's uncle Peter to drive to Steinbach, Manitoba, a Mennonite town quickly gaining a reputation as the regional "automobile city" and the home of his sister Aganetha.

She had married Peter B. Reimer in 1934, which John knew about from some of the last letters they had received while he was still in Siberia. Peter was a farmer and, in the 1950s, quite successful. The Reimer family had been members of a subgroup of Mennonites known as the Kleine Gemeinde that had settled in the Steinbach area. As a result of a church split, another group, known as Holdeman, had been formed, and some time before my parents arrived in Steinbach Peter had joined that group. The Holdeman church had a large following in the Steinbach area, and their characteristic beards for baptized males and black head coverings for women made them readily visible in the community. Aganetha was mother to twelve children, and a reserved nature together with her husband's increasing religious eccentricity meant the divergence of her life experiences from those of her brother was extraordinary.

John travelled to Steinbach and stayed at his sister's farm for a month while he looked for work. He got a job at an auto dealer as a mechanic, a job more suited to him than farming. For Margaret, the time John was away was lonely. She felt responsible for the whole family and was gradually running out of money. Her story of adjusting to a new life in Canada included an account of a lady who appeared at her door to collect money for the Red Cross. Margaret had only a dime left but was too embarrassed not to give the woman anything. So she gave her the dime. That evening John came back from Steinbach with the proceeds of his first paycheque. After a few days in Drake, he returned to Steinbach alone to work and find accommodations for the family.

When John returned to Steinbach, he tried to buy a house. In one of his stories, he recalled asking his brother-in-law Peter for a loan to make the down payment. Peter took him down into the basement of their farm home, reached up between the floor joists, took down a bag, and counted out $500. This was unimaginable wealth for John. Trying to borrow the rest from the local credit union was impossible; he had no credit record and no equity. Negotiating with the seller to take back a mortgage did work out, however, and within a month or two the groundwork had been laid for a new beginning. In April 1954, John returned to Drake to pick up the family, and a day after his arrival their second child, another son, was born. The move to Steinbach now included an extended family made up of John and Margaret, who were thirty-six and thirty-two, and their two children, one of whom was a newborn and the other aged one and a half; Margaret's parents, who were seventy and eighty-three; and Marie and Erwin Vogt, Tina's children, who were thirteen and fifteen.

Meshed with stories of hardship were stories of the humorous side of adjusting to a new country. John was driving his pickup truck when he came upon a skunk on the road. Not being familiar with skunks, he had not worried unduly about avoiding it and accidentally drove over it, only to experience the pungent smell familiar to all rural prairie folk. He tried unsuccessfully to wash the truck and finally had to park it in a gravel pit near Steinbach for two weeks until the smell had dissipated enough that he could live with it.

Until Erwin and Marie could begin work, John was the only wage earner, and it meant careful management of the household and hard work in the garden and kitchen on Margaret's part. Nevertheless, the move to Steinbach was a crucial turning point for the Werners. The dramatic increase in automobile ownership that characterized the 1950s and 1960s boded well for John's skills and Steinbach automobile dealers. With relatively consistent employment, John and Margaret could make the mortgage payments on the house that John had bought on Main Street at the edge of town. They joined the Steinbach Mennonite Church, whose members were in large part Mennonite immigrants who had come to Canada from the Soviet Union in the 1920s. The church helped to supplement the income needed to support Margaret's elderly parents until her mother had been a resident for ten years and became eligible for Old Age Security.

Another cycle of autobiographical memory began with my first memories: the memory of my grandfather taking me by the hand to watch equipment digging a hole for a new water treatment facility near our home and then the memory of how he became ill and his death in 1957 when I was five. John and Margaret also continued to be parents to the two orphaned children. As a fifteen year old, Erwin had more developed connections to Drake, and when he got his driver's licence he went back, but according to my mother he came back with tattered clothes and no money. Marie was much more conscious of being an immigrant and worked hard helping my brothers and me with schoolwork.

Four years after John and Margaret arrived in Steinbach, the federal government created the Canada Mortgage and Housing Corporation (CMHC) mortgage program, which meant they could buy a new home in one of Steinbach's first postwar suburbs, with a low down payment and a long time to pay off the mortgage. They were like most other postwar Canadian couples who had a strong desire for family and household security. They raised six children in the bungalow they had built on Spruce Crescent.

Margaret contributed to the household economy with a large garden and jars of canning that filled the pantry each fall. Picking blueberries in the forests of the Canadian Shield was an annual ritual whose tediousness was tempered by the prospect of eating the Mennonite version of perogies my mother made that was a frequent treat during the winter. The garden was contested space in my parents' relationship. In the early years of living in the home on Spruce Crescent, the back yard was almost entirely devoted to the garden, and almost all of it was planted to vegetables. For my mother, the memories of the famine loomed large, and she placed great importance on the ability to raise your own food. Each spring my father would negotiate for more lawn and less garden, an idea my mother steadfastly resisted. Gradually, however, the grass took over the garden, and more flowers appeared, but there was always a garden. Late summer and fall were busy with picking, shelling, peeling, and canning. A kitchen full of home-baked buns and lemon twists on Saturday mornings also helped to moderate the size of the food budget needed for the large family.

It took a few years before "Canadian" foods entered the Werner household. The arrival of pizza, which some of my siblings had tasted at friends' homes, was nearly a traumatic event. My mother was sure the pungent smell of baked cheese signalled that whatever it was it had spoiled. Toast, on the other hand, she tasted for the first time in the hospital after one of my siblings was born. It meant that we soon acquired a toaster, and though the bread remained home baked rather than the "Wonder Bread" popular in the 1960s it was now toasted.

When John first began work in Steinbach, he worked for an automobile dealer who also owned a construction company. His stories included driving a caterpillar and scraper constructing drains on the flat lake bottom of Manitoba's Red River Valley. For the most part, however, he fixed cars. For a decade or more, John supplemented his day job by buying used cars, fixing them up after his regular working hours at one of Steinbach's automobile dealerships, and then selling them. A series of six or seven 1952 and 1953 Chevrolets briefly became the family car before being sold at a profit, only to be followed by the next one that needed some repairs. There was not a lot of time for anything other than work; John worked long hours, many evenings, and every Saturday.

Recreation for a growing immigrant family had to be inexpensive. An outing on Sunday after church was a picnic in the park. The Werner family joined other immigrant families in Winnipeg's Assiniboine Park. In the 1950s and early 1960s, a variety of immigrant families used the park for a summer afternoon away from the daily routines and grind of finding their way into the middle class. After a few years in Steinbach, John took up fishing and, as time and resources permitted, was able to make fishing a lasting and enjoyable hobby. Family trips began to include Sunday afternoons to one of Manitoba's many lakes, and picnics came to be replaced by overnight camping trips.

Living in what was then a predominantly Mennonite community meant that John and Margaret could attend German church, and the language of the workplace and for most other things they needed could be Low German. As a result, they never became as fluent in English as did most of their postwar immigrant counterparts. The family doctor, Dr. Krueger, spoke fluent High German, and most businesses had staff fluent in Mennonite Low German. Being the oldest in the family, I have sharp, and not always pleasant, memories of having to take or make phone calls for my parents when there was an English-only speaker at the other end of the line or facing the obligation of reading and explaining mail that was unanticipated or unusual. I have no memories of learning to speak English. Although Mennonite Low German was the only language spoken in the home, I somehow learned English— apparently first from playing with the neighbourhood children and then in school. In contrast to most Mennonites in Steinbach, it was important in our family to be German Mennonites. It meant attending German-language Saturday school, where Pastor Hulseman from the local Lutheran church tried desperately to convey the German language to his reluctant, blond-haired, blue-eyed, and freckle-faced charges. For Margaret, the increasing use of English among her children was a lasting disappointment, and her inability to converse easily with her grandchildren was the clearest sign of the challenges she faced adapting to a new country.

The adjustment of my parents to Canadian life, though not traumatic, was a constant reality in our home. I recall with some guilt being embarrassed about my parents—particularly about their poor English-language skills. I do not recall any conversations about returning to Germany and certainly not to the Soviet Union. After I became an adult, there were treasured visits to Germany but only because of the connection to relatives from their "old world." Modern Germany had little appeal for them and was really a foreign country. There were differences between my parents, my father was much less likely to look back, but it took my mother almost to the end of her life to admit that her home was now Canada.

Memories, Stories, and History

THE WAR YEARS WASHED OVER MY PARENTS' LIVES like a tsunami, and the debris left in its wake resurfaced in the 1950s. Much, however, was gone forever. The MCC's search service continued to function well into the 1950s to try to reconnect families torn apart by the war. Along with placing a request with the MCC, Margaret posted notices in the German-language Mennonite paper *Der Bote* to try to find John's sisters in the Soviet Union. Sometime in the 1950s, his sister in Siberia heard from an acquaintance about the request and responded. After having heard no news about each other for fifteen years, the story of their experiences after John left in 1938 began to emerge.

His sisters and mother had received no news of his whereabouts after their last letters. After the attack by Germany in 1941, life had become steadily more difficult. Like many other women, Katya and Martha were conscripted into Stalin's work army, the *trudarmiya*. Food became ever scarcer, and at the height of the pressure on the Soviet Union in 1943 John's mother, Anna Janzen, died. She had gradually become weaker due to the extreme deprivation of the war years—essentially she starved. When I visited Tante Katya in Germany in the 1990s, she recalled how they could not find anyone to dig a grave for her in the frozen ground. Her body was kept frozen in the unheated pantry until the spring thaw allowed for and required burial. Even then she was buried on top of another body in a recently dug grave because the ground was still too frozen and no one had the strength to dig a new grave. After the strict regulations preventing Soviet Germans from moving were lifted in 1955, Katya and her husband Johan Moos moved to Karaganda and then Dzambul in Kazakhstan, an area with warmer weather and easier life. Her sister Martha soon followed. Letters from Katya and Martha throughout the 1960s focussed on their physical needs, and there were frequent requests to send clothing. John and Margaret and John's sister and brother-in-law sent parcels to them to alleviate his sisters' needs. Martha moved to East Germany when the opportunity came in the early 1980s, and with the advent of glasnost and perestroika in the late 1980s both sisters and their families moved to Darmstadt in West Germany.

The villages where my father grew up also disappeared. In 1951, the four collective villages that made up the Pashnaya settlement, including Markovka and Grigorevka, were merged into the Ananyewka collective farm, and in 1971 both villages were eliminated.[1] By the time I visited the Slavgorod area in 2010, all that was left of Grigorevka and Markovka were the outlines of a village street, a clump of small trees that signalled where a cemetery had been, and a grassed area with a few bricks sticking out here and there. People living in nearby Ananyewka had only vague memories of what had once been and remembered only that the people living there had been moved to larger nearby villages but not when.

John's first wife never remarried. According to Katya, she had accepted the reality of the turmoil of the war years and the news that he had survived the war and was in Canada. She died in the Soviet Union in 1986 before emigration to Germany became a possibility for large numbers of Soviet Germans. She and John never corresponded. Margaret's husband Peter Vogt also survived the war. By the time a mutual relative advised Margaret in the 1950s that he was alive in East Germany, he had remarried and had a family. In interviews with my mother, she only commented that it would have been good to tell him how difficult it had been to face the refugee experience and loss of their child alone.

Margaret's brother Jacob, drafted into the German Army in the last months of the war, was never heard from again. Searches in the records of German organizations dedicated to locating records or graves of former German soldiers were unsuccessful. Not knowing what finally happened to her brother and the nagging thought that he might be alive somewhere comprised a source of grief for the rest of Margaret's life. Julius Vogt, her half-sister's husband, who had been sent east in 1941, also survived, and by the time his children reconnected with him he had married a Russian woman and had three children. He was living in the town of Berezniki in the Ural Mountains north of the city of Perm. He died soon after they found each other, and the last letter they received was from the oldest child, who wrote to them in Russian.[2] Osterwick in Ukraine, where Margaret grew up, lived long in her memory and to some extent became an idealized memory of her real home. Canada remained a foreign country to her for many years. That began to change when a family friend from Osterwick went back to the village when doing so became possible. His photos made her realize that the image of Osterwick she held on to was only a memory, and she began a gradual, though never complete, adjustment to Canada.

Hints of more wreckage of the war years surfaced in the 1950s. After my father died, there was a story about a letter arriving in the 1950s or 1960s from a woman with whom John had had a relationship and how Margaret had opened and read it. There was also a story about a woman with a young boy who had arrived at John's sister's home looking for John, claiming he was the father of her son. These mysterious hints of more untold stories surfaced briefly but were never talked about again.

For John, stories of beginning again in Canada were less important than the overriding story of the war experience. Gradually, however, that changed. It seemed that telling and retelling the stories was therapeutic, and slowly the need to tell them again faded. The need to tell them also diminished as the war years receded from the lived memory of most of the people he came in contact with.

What did my father remember, how did he reconstruct those memories into stories, and how do they relate to history? These are the questions that have appeared and reappeared throughout this book. Although not my primary interest, a vast body of psychological and neurological inquiry attempts to answer the question of how we actually remember and forget. The basic state of this research, as it pertains to my family's memories, can be summarized as follows. After age three or four, we begin to acquire autobiographical memories and can remember and tell others about things that have happened to us. What we remember is influenced by many things. There is a sense that we decide during, or shortly after, events whether or not they are memorable, and then we script and rehearse these memories internally and externally in the form of stories we tell others. These memories acquire a certain permanence and vary little after this initial period of formation.[3] There is a primacy effect in our retention of the details of life events. Even for a soldier, the first occurrence of a life-threatening experience can overshadow similarly dangerous events, and they can be forgotten. Many other factors confound our memories, distorting them or even creating completely false memories. Interference by competing emotions or preoccupations causes us to forget, while the intensity of experience often enhances the vividness of memory but not necessarily its accuracy. Occasionally we might retain an almost visual memory, sometimes called "flash bulb" memories, that while vivid can also be inaccurate.[4] Our memories become distorted in a variety of ways. We suffer from source amnesia, or we remember something but confuse the source of the memory, recalling something we saw in a film or read in a newspaper as if it was our own experience.[5] Our memories distort time, often lengthening periods of time in which we have particularly vivid memories and shortening the times of events that we remember only slightly.[6]

We not only have memories of our past lives, but our memories also become autobiographical when shared with others as stories. As developmental psychologist Susan Engels puts it, "the more one has communicated a given memory, the more it becomes a story."[7] Attempts to understand the process of converting memories into stories have often led to the creation of metaphors. The earliest metaphor was that memory is like writing—Plato's notion that memory is like a wax tablet on which perceptions and thoughts are stamped like the impression made by an object on wax. There were other ancient metaphors for memory. In his *Confessions,* written in the fourth century and believed to be the first autobiography, Augustine talks about palaces of memory, where "memories of earlier events give way to those which followed, and as they pass are stored away available when I want them." In these halls of memory, he says, "I meet myself and recall what I am, what I have done and when and how I was affected when I did it."[8] The advent of photography led to its use as a metaphor for memory, and the expression "photographic memory" came to be used for people who had an almost abnormal ability to recall visually based memories. Successive technological developments led to metaphors likening memory to a tape recorder and then to video and the magnetic memory of computer storage media. None of these, as Ulrich Neisser points out, captures the complexity of memory.[9]

Aware of the limitations of using metaphor to explain memory, I think there is a metaphor that has some resonance with how autobiographical memory functioned for my father and the way he told, and did not tell, stories. Its application is limited to autobiographical or episodic memory, since it was orally transmitted, not semantic memory, as in our ability to recall facts and general knowledge of the world.

Imagine autobiographical memory as the building blocks children play with to build a small spaceship, a farm wagon, or a fireman. These blocks are the fragments of memory from my father's past. They are stored in small drawers such as those found in the hardware section of a store where various kinds of fasteners are displayed. Near the wall of these drawers is a card index; written on each card is the location of each block or memory fragment. When my father told stories, he accessed the card index to locate certain memory fragments, which he then built into modules or stories. As Geoffrey Cubitt suggests, the process "is always somewhat of a speculative navigational labour,"[10] so my father's stories were creative reconstructions built from fragments of memory that could be located. The modules became part of a larger image that my father constructed using other modules that together created a building block version of himself. Pieces that did not fit with the image that he wanted to portray were not used. Sometimes completed modules were stored in the drawers as memory chunks rather than individual fragments. They could be accessed in their entirety with only minor modifications.

This metaphor has limitations. In particular, it suggests that memory fragments are discrete, like building blocks. The metaphor also imbues memory fragments with stability and suggests that recall is formulaic and reproducible. Research related to memory suggests that the memories we store are much more fluid and amorphous and sometimes called up unconsciously by stimuli such as smell, sight, and verbal association. As neuroscientist Steven Rose points out, "there is no single site for 'the memory' as if it constituted a discrete entity," and "each act of recall is itself a new experience."[11]

The metaphor does point, however, to some of the characteristics of my father's autobiographical memory. Cards in the index were sometimes misplaced or fell to the floor, and for a time, even while the memory fragments remained in place, they were inaccessible or when put back were in different places. As the English writer Cyril Connolly said, "our memories are card indexes consulted, and then put back in disorder by authorities whom we do not control."[12] Sometimes blocks were added to the collection that did not belong there. They became part of the inventory of memory fragments stored as my father's even though they came through reading the newspaper, watching propaganda newsreels, or listening to the accounts of others and not from his own experience. The story of his being present when Hermann Goering told his accusers at the Nuremberg trials that they would not have the opportunity to hang him is the clearest example of substituted memory in my father's stories. Some blocks were safely stored in the drawers but never "played with." These memory fragments could not be put together into stories in ways that did not violate the image my father wanted to project, or there was no audience to whom they could be entrusted. He demonstrated considerable creativity in constructing extensive and detailed narratives of his life experiences without mentioning relationships with women, including a wife, before he met my mother. It seems meeting and marrying my mother compromised these memories, rendering them untellable. Of course, many blocks were lost or intentionally discarded or forgotten. Keeping all of the memories would have exceeded the storage capacity of the drawer, and using them would have created "cognitive overloading that would...prevent the mind from making usable sense of anything."[13]

More important to a discussion of autobiography's relationship to history is understanding why my father told stories the way he did. What influenced the building block version of himself he wanted to portray, and how did the way he told stories contribute to that image? As Jill Ker Conway argues, long-standing gendered conventions have framed the writing of autobiography and might apply to unwritten autobiography in the form of oral history. The "overarching pattern" for men is that "life is an odyssey, a journey through many trials and tests, which the hero must surmount alone through courage, endurance, cunning and moral strength."[14] Women's autobiography, meanwhile, has been characterized by the dominant theme of women as the "romantic heroine" with "no agency, or power to act on her own behalf."[15]

Although the romantic heroine motif is really not apparent in the two narratives by women in this book, my mother and Tina Hinz conveyed a different sense of agency in their stories. My mother's story of famine and hunger, first in the Soviet Union in 1933 and then after the war, focussed on her inability to change anything and the helplessness of being dependent on the goodwill of others, while my father's story of the 1933 famine dwelt on his initiative and the risks he took to find food on the steppes. Conway also suggests that the acceptable narrative for women has been to frame the story in relation to God. Like the autobiographies of medieval Christian women mystics, both my mother and my aunt Tina relied on religious imagery or, as Conway notes, "a relationship with a first cause" instead of their own agency to narrate the events of their lives.[16] In contrast to my mother's stories, there were elements of the heroic odyssey in my father's stories. It was my father who took the wounded German soldiers to the field hospital and who pulled the truck through the river in the middle of Montgomery's assault on the Rhine. He provided empathy and closure for his friend's grieving parents, he was there to help the Jewish student escape certain death when he was to appear before the naturalization commissions in occupied Poland, and he advised the politruk in the POW camp near Minsk how to save himself.

In addition to established patterns and models of how men and women tell stories, the assembly of memory modules into stories is shaped by social context. My father's stories as I heard and recorded them were told from the point of view of an immigrant to Canada. The Soviet and Nazi powers, which my father had served, were remarkably transformed in the mentality of the postwar period. The Soviet former ally was now the Cold War enemy, while Germany, the home of Nazi ideology, was being integrated into the "right" side of the Soviet–East and U.S.–West dichotomy. My father's narrative followed the broader historical narratives. It was benign in telling the story of the near suffocation on the U.S. Army POW train, transferring the fault for most of the mistreatment my father suffered to African Americans or the French. His coming to terms with the Soviet system as one in which he could get ahead must also be inferred and was never explicit. It is interesting to contemplate how the narrative would have changed had he not come to Canada but stayed in Germany as Johann or had he been repatriated to the Soviet Union and become Ivan again.

The context that most clearly shaped my father's stories was the religious and cultural milieu of his postwar home in Steinbach. For Mennonite women, as Marlene Epp argues, stories of war, the refugee experience, and subsequent immigration to Canada "do not fit into the accepted Mennonite narrative" and hence "may become submerged and even lost in the effort to preserve the social memory of the group." In spite of the traditional Mennonite emphasis on pacifism, Epp suggests that men's "wartime experiences presented an intellectual and theological dilemma that fitted into accepted categories."[17] In many ways, however, the Mennonite pacifist position necessarily legitimized suffering for one's belief and denied impulses to protect person and property using violence. Both my mother and my aunt Tina cast their stories within an overall narrative of suffering even though in many instances they demonstrated agency to the point of heroism. Stories of participation in killing during combat, however, were not acceptable narratives for Mennonite audiences. My father's stories responded to this reality of his social context by focussing almost entirely on what was done to him rather than placing him in the centre of what his wartime activities did to others. The clearest examples were the gaps in his story about the Finnish war. Military accounts suggest that tank drivers were credited with breaking through the Mannerheim Line with, one must assume, considerable loss of life. Johann was a tank driver, but there were no stories about these events or indeed almost the entire period of his combat during the Winter War.

But is my father's narrative history? Personal memories and their conversion by the telling of stories into autobiographies, oral narratives, and memoirs have been controversial as legitimate contributions to history. David Thelen, observing a roundtable discussion involving historians who had experienced the Second World War, noted that most considered their own memories to be "a time-out from real history."[18] The debate about personal narratives in relation to historical narratives has often been polarized. Oral history can be useful in providing "contextual details that personalized historical processes," as Roger Horowitz has noted. It can also provide colour but "not narrative structure."[19] Others suggest that oral narratives can help to "order the actual course of events," as Forrest Pogue, an early oral historian and interviewer of American soldiers in the Second World War, maintained.[20]

The importance of oral narratives in twenty-first-century historical discussion, to a large extent, is an attempt to democratize history. As Geoffrey Cubitt notes, "'memory' designates the multiple and disorganized, but always potentially resurgent, voices of the marginalized or excluded."[21] Stories of individual experiences, with the contradictions and impossible or irrational choices that life brings, are a necessary check on the dominant narratives told in histories that rely on documents left behind by leaders and politicians. My father's stories are a counterpoint to the dominant narratives of the Second World War from a Western perspective. They resist the simple categorizations of Germans as perpetrators, Allies as saviours, or national identity as singular and largely immutable. Even in a much narrower Mennonite context, they challenge the given understanding that Stalin's Soviet Union was universally antithetical to Mennonite sensibilities.

My parents' stories illustrated the multiple intersections and layering of scale inherent in telling stories about the past. As individuals, we participate in the history of our time on a small scale. Despite his remarkable flurry of experiences, my father participated in very little of what would be the story of Stalin, the Second World War, and postwar immigration to Canada. However, both my parents framed their stories in constant tension with what became the dominant Western narrative during the Cold War. Although they experienced famine, war, the Holocaust, and dislocation, they could not have known the places of these events in the later master narrative, and they could not avoid telling their stories in relation to that narrative. I finally had to stop engaging my mother in conversations about the treatment of Jews, the Nazi occupation, and Hitler because she believed my sense of the story was coloured by the Canadian history view. Her rejoinder was that "you had to be there."

My father's autobiography also recalls the tensions his stories created for a boy growing up in postwar suburban Canada. Although I do not recall his answer, I remember asking my father why he was not on parade when the few veterans in Steinbach marched to the cenotaph at the town's main inter-section on Remembrance Day. It took me some time to grasp that, though Remembrance Day honoured those who had served and died in the war, not all who had served and died were to be remembered in the same way. As I be-gan to grasp the gravity of the Holocaust, I remember experiencing a moment of fear that there would be a knock on the door and that my father would be arrested for having committed an atrocity—a story that he had never told us.

Finally, the stories told here offer a remarkable commentary on the human spirit and resilience with which we deal with conflicting and compromising memories. Reflecting on what her sister has told her, the narrator in Marina Lewycka's humorous but thought-provoking novel *A Short History of Tractors in Ukrainian* acknowledges that "some things are better not known, for the knowledge of them can never be unknown." Once I knew my father's secrets, they could not become unknown. The novel's humour comes from the second marriage of her elderly father to a much younger gold digger, but a subtheme of the novel is an earlier dark family secret. The narrator is astounded by her parents' ability to go on with life despite difficult memories and a "terrible secret" and wonders how "they grow vegetables, and mend motor-bikes, and send us to school and worry about our exam results? But they did."[22] I sometimes thought my father would be unable to come to terms with his memories and suffer some kind of mental breakdown as a result. The opposite happened. Not only did he continue to fix motorbikes, but also he gradually told his stories less often and with less urgency. He was able to assemble his narrative—to fix his spoiled biography—in ways that allowed him to come to terms with his past.

Appendix: Family Trees

Werner–Janzen–Froese Family

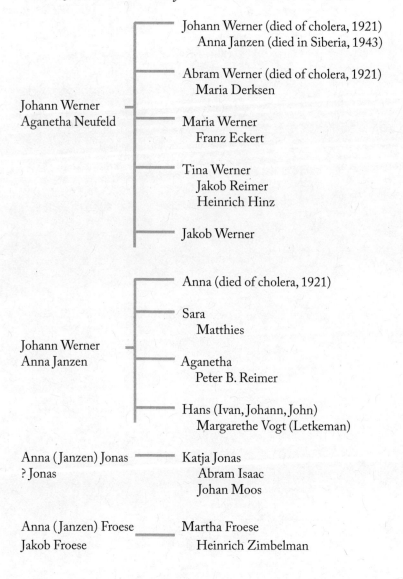

Johann Werner / Aganetha Neufeld

- Johann Werner (died of cholera, 1921)
  Anna Janzen (died in Siberia, 1943)
- Abram Werner (died of cholera, 1921)
  Maria Derksen
- Maria Werner
  Franz Eckert
- Tina Werner
  Jakob Reimer
  Heinrich Hinz
- Jakob Werner

Johann Werner / Anna Janzen

- Anna (died of cholera, 1921)
- Sara
  Matthies
- Aganetha
  Peter B. Reimer
- Hans (Ivan, Johann, John)
  Margarethe Vogt (Letkeman)

Anna (Janzen) Jonas / ? Jonas

- Katja Jonas
  Abram Isaac
  Johan Moos

Anna (Janzen) Froese / Jakob Froese

- Martha Froese
  Heinrich Zimbelman

Werner–Letkeman Family

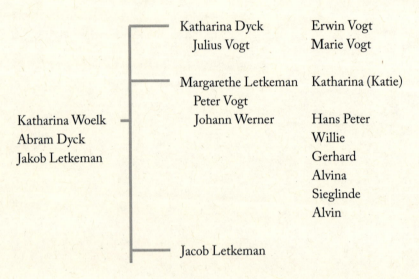

Katharina Dyck   Erwin Vogt
Julius Vogt   Marie Vogt

Margarethe Letkeman   Katharina (Katie)
Peter Vogt
Johann Werner   Hans Peter
                          Willie
Katharina Woelk   Gerhard
Abram Dyck   Alvina
Jakob Letkeman   Sieglinde
                          Alvin

Jacob Letkeman

Note: Only family members who appeared in my father's stories are listed
     here.

Glossary

Afrika Korps	the German Army in Africa
Alexsandrovka	a village in the concentrated German settlement area northeast of Slavgorod
Angerapp, Angerab, Ozyorsk	a city in the Russian federation, formerly East Prussia, entered as Johann Werner's birthplace by the German Army
Annanyevka	one of the Pashnaya villages and the location of the *selsoviet*
artel	a collective farm where the peasants kept their own yards but pooled all their equipment, fields, and farm work
Pabiance, Pabianitz, Babianitz	a town just outside Litzmannstadt
Barnaul	a city along the Ob River in West Siberia
blitzmädchen	young women enlisted for various services in support of the German war effort. The name came from the lightning bolt patch worn by women who worked as radio operators.
brigadier	the highest management position in a collective farm
Cherno Dol	a Ukrainian village near the concentrated German settlement area northeast of Slavgorod
Choroschoje, Khoroshee	one of the Eighties Villages, also known as number eighty-seven
Chortitza, Khortitza	the first or Old Colony established by Mennonites at the junction of the Dnieper and Chortitza Rivers in Ukraine in 1789. One of the villages was also named Chortitza.
combinyor	a combine operator in the machine tractor station (MTS) system
dachas	the summer homes surrounding Moscow
desyatin	a unit of land area in tsarist times equal to 2.7 acres or 1.1 hectares
dummkopf	an idiot

Eighties Villages	a cluster of villages located about fifty kilometres southeast of the concentrated German settlement area northeast of Slavgorod
Ekaterinoslav	the tsarist-era province where the Old Colony was located
Esbit	a solid fuel made of hexamine invented in Germany in 1936 and used in military field stoves
Étain	a town in France west of Metz; site of a POW camp
EWZ Einwandererzentralstelle	the German organization that processed ethnic Germans for citizenship
Fabrikerwiese	a village in the Molotschna Colony
Fiseler Storch	a light reconnaissance and air ambulance airplane used by the German Army
gefreiter	German military rank equivalent to lance corporal
GPU (or OGPU)	the state political directorate under the Soviet system responsible for security and the persecution of religious groups
Grodno	a city in Poland on the German–Russian frontier in 1941; misspelled by my father as Grodnau in some documents
Grigorevka, Grigorewka	one of the Pashnaya villages
Nekrasovo, Halbstadt	a village and the administrative centre of the concentrated German settlement area northeast of Slavgorod
herrenvolk	the master race, the superior Aryan race of Nazi ideology
jabos	the German nickname for Allied fighter–bombers
Kanzerovka	a Ukrainian town on the rail line near the Chortitza Colony
kaserne	a military compound or base
Kirchliche	the larger church grouping among Russian Mennonites; also referred to here as the Kirchengemeinde
Kitchkas	the former village of Einlage in the Chortitza Colony
Klyuchia	a Russian village not far from the Pashnaya villages in Siberia
kolkhoz	a collective farm
kulak	literally "fist." The term referred to peasants deemed to be "exploiters," who were banished or executed; the drive to eliminate kulaks was known as "dekulakization."

Kulunda	the name of the steppe in the Slavgorod area of West Siberia; also the name of a town south of Slavgorod
Lebensraum	literally "living space." It was Hitler's grand scheme to create space for German expansion in Eastern Europe by conquest and resettlement.
Litzmannstadt, Łódź	a city in Poland that was the major centre for processing ethnic German migrants during the German occupation
Luftwaffe	the German Air Force
Mailly-le-Camp	a French village about 220 kilometres east of Paris and the site of a large POW camp
Markovka, Markow	one of the Pashnaya villages
mladshiy leytenant	a rank designation in the Red Army equivalent to a junior lieutenant
Molotschna	the name of the second colony established by Mennonites in 1803; also the name of the river along which the colony was established
Moskalenki, Moskalenka	a village east of Omsk along the Trans-Siberian Railway
MTS	machine tractor stations. The MTS was a second-level collective that provided mechanized services to the kolkhoz farms.
Nadarovka	a Mennonite village near Pavlodar in Siberia
nebelwerfer	a rocket launcher
Niederwampach	a village in Belgium near Bastogne
Nikolaipol, Nikol'skiy	a Mennonite village in the concentrated German settlement area northeast of the city of Slavgorod
NSKK	Nationalsozialistischeskraftfahrerkorps, a Nazi party organization devoted to training for and providing transport services
Oberwampach	a village in Belgium near Bastogne
ostarbeiter	forced labour taken from Eastern Europe by the Germans to work in German factories
Osterwick	a Mennonite village in the Chortitza Colony
OT	Organization Todt, devoted to supporting the military by constructing roads, bridges, and other infrastructure
panzer	tank or armoured military vehicle. Panzer divisions and armies were mechanized units of the German Army.
Panzerspeewagon	a light armoured vehicle

Pashnaya	a cluster of Mennonite villages located about 100 kilometres southeast of the concentrated German settlement northeast of Slavgorod
Perlovka	a train station and suburb of 1929 Moscow
Podsosnovo	a Lutheran village on the northern edge of the concentrated German settlement area northeast of the city of Slavgorod
politruk	a political commissar attached to Red Army units to assure adequate party vigilance and control over the military
polta	a traditional evening celebrating a couple's engagement. Guests also brought gifts for the couple.
pud	a unit of weight during the tsarist era; 1 *pud* = 16.3 kilograms
RAD	Reichsarbeitsdienst, a German labour organization
Reichswald	a forested area on the west bank of the Rhine River north of the German city of Xanten
Reinfeld	a Mennonite village in the concentrated German settlement area northeast of Slavgorod
Rhinewiesenlager	large, open-air, fenced enclosures built by the U.S. Army in which the large numbers of captured and surrendering German soldiers were temporarily put. Conditions in these enclosures were very difficult.
RKFDV	Reichskommissariat fur die Festigung des Deutschen Volkstums, an organization devoted to preserving the German character and purity of ethnic Germans
samohonka	homemade, distilled liquor—moonshine
Schnee Eiffel	the Ardennes forest along the German–Belgian border
Schoenberg	a Mennonite village in the Chortitza Colony
Schwerpunkt Artillerie	the artillery units whose task was to fire on the point of attack, either while attacking or defending
selsoviet	the equivalent of a local government office under the Soviet system
Silberfeld, Serebropol	a Mennonite village in the cluster of villages known as the Eighties Villages
Skvortsovka, Skworzowo	a village south of the Trans-Siberian Railway near Petropavlovsk

SS	*Schutz Staffel.* Originally Hitler's bodyguards, the SS became part of the German war machine with its own command structure and referred to as the Waffen SS.
Stakhanovite	a person who exceeded the norms set out by the state for work performance. Stakhanovites were rewarded by the state with honours and special privileges.
stellungsbefehl	a German military draft order
Taurida	the tsarist-era province where the Molotschna Colony was located
Torgsin	stores where foreigners and party officials could buy consumer goods otherwise not generally available provided they had access to hard currency
Totenkopf	a notorious SS division of the German military
TOZ	a collective farm where only the fieldwork was done together
tractorist	a tractor operator in the machine tractor station (MTS) system
trossraum	the rear area for a German military unit where supplies were assembled and repairs and other support operations were performed
trudanye	a labour day; a unit of work on a collective farm that formed the basis for compensation for its members
trudarmiya	a work army created by Stalin
verst	a tsarist-era unit of distance equal to 1.067 kilometres
vertrauensmänner	contact persons for the MCC who kept lists of refugees and acted as liaisons between refugees and the organization
Vlasov Army	a military unit made up of former Red Army soldiers who fought on the German side. They were led by General Andrei Vlasov, a former Red Army general.
volksliste	the Nazi list placing ethnic Germans into categories based on their suitability for membership in the master race
Volkssturm	an adhoc marshalling of young boys and old men to defend German cities against Allied invaders in the last months of the Second World War
VoMi	Volksdeutsche Mittelstelle, an SS organization dedicated to integrating ethnic Germans into Nazi Germany

Wehrkreis	a military district used to recruit replacements for specific military units
Wehrmacht	the regular German Army
Wochenschau	a weekly propaganda reel shown in German theatres before the main feature
Zagradovka	one of the Mennonite colonies in Ukraine, located southwest of the city of Zaporozhye
Zlatopolye	a town between Kulunda and the Pashnaya villages in Siberia
Zugmaschine	a half-track used by the German Army to pull cannons

Notes

Introduction

1 David Thelen, "An Afterthought on Scale and History," *Journal of American History* 77, 2 (1990): 592.

2 Susan Engel, *Context Is Everything: The Nature of Memory* (New York: Freeman, 1999), 157; Art Spiegelman, *Maus: A Survivor's Tale* (New York: Pantheon Books, 1997).

3 Endel Tulving, "Episodic Memory and Common Sense: How Far Apart?," in *Episodic Memory: New Directions in Research*, ed. Alan Baddely, Martin Conway, and John Aggleton (Oxford: Oxford University Press, 2002), 270.

4 Ulrich Neisser, "Memory with a Grain of Salt," in *Memory: An Anthology*, ed. Harriet Harvey Wood and A.S. Byatt (London: Vintage, 2009), 88.

5 Engel, *Context Is Everything*, 83.

6 Jill Ker Conway, *When Memory Speaks: Exploring the Art of Autobiography* (Toronto: Random House, 1998), 177.

7 Tina Hinz, "Memoir," (Paderborn: n.p., 1968). The memoir was subsequently transcribed, edited, and privately printed by the Hinz family. The original handwritten and printed versions form the basis of the following account. The page numbers are from the printed version.

Chapter 1: Beginnings

1 Serebropol in Russian.

2 Tina Hinz, "Memoir," (Paderborn: n.p., 1968), 81; John Werner, interview tape 1, 22 March 1987.

3 Hans Mansson, "Childhood Stuttering: Incidence and Development," *Journal of Fluency Disorders* 25, 1 (2000): 47–57.

4 Helmut Anger, *Die Deutschen in Sibierien: Reise durch die deutschen Dörfer Westsibiriens* (Berlin: Ost-Europa Verlag, 1930), 38–39. Average yields in the Kulunda Steppe were 4.0 bushels per acre in 1920, 5.0 in 1921 and 1922, 2.7 in 1923, and only 2.1 in 1924. Quoted in Manfred Klaube, *Die Deutschen Dörfer in der Westsibirischen Kulunda-Steppe: Entwicklung, Strukturen, Probleme* (Marburg: N.G. Elwert Verlag, 1991), 44. A letter from my grandmother in the 1930s suggested they had obtained eleven bushels per acre. Anna Janzen, letter fragment #7, n.d.

5 EWZ record card number 723 213, undated, Berlin Document Centre (hereafter BDC).

6   Geoffrey Cubitt, *History and Memory* (Manchester: Manchester University Press, 2007), 128.

Chapter 2: Difficult Years

1   Manfred Klaube, *Die Deutschen Dörfer in der Westsibirischen Kulunda-Steppe: Entwicklung, Strukturen, Probleme* (Marburg: N.G. Elwert Verlag, 1991), 45.

2   In Low German, his nickname was Schacha Jaunse. Schacha is an expression that alludes to the game of chess. In this context, it refers to his dealing or trading.

3   Mennonite Heritage Centre Archives (hereafter MHC), Winnipeg, Canadian Mennonite Board of Colonization (hereafter CMBC), vol. 3393.

4   Letter to Aganetha dated 22 February 1927, OS (Old Style), from a collection kept by Aganetha's son Willie Reimer and loaned to me by Maxine Fehr, his daughter. The reference to "Eighty-Six" is to the village of Silberfeld, where the Janzens lived.

5   Martha Zimbelman, *Lebenslauf,* personal communication, n.d. The account written by Martha suffers from numerous inaccuracies. She conflates the emigration of the Aaron Janzens (1925) and the attempted emigration of the Johan Froeses (1929). Hers is also the only account suggesting that Aaron might have consulted with his sister about taking Aganetha with them on the basis that they would soon follow.

6   Aganetha Reimer, obituary, Blumenort, MB.

7   Anna Janzen, letter fragment #8, 22 February 1927, OS.

8   Ibid.; Anna Janzen, letter fragment #5, n.d. The content of the letter points to its having been written in May, 1928.

9   Anna Janzen, letter fragment #5, n.d.

10   Anna Janzen, letter fragment #2, 20 February 1929, OS.

11   Harvey L. Dyck, "Collectivization, Depression, and Immigration, 1929–1930: A Chance Interplay," in *Empire and Nations: Essays in Honour of Frederic H. Soward,* ed. Harvey L. Dyck and H. Peter Krosby (Toronto: University of Toronto Press, 1969), 144–59; H.J. Wilms, comp., *Vor den Toren Moskaus* (Abbotsford, BC: Committee of the Mennonite Refugees from the Soviet Union, 1960).

12   John Werner, interview tape 6, Summer, 1988.

13   Frank H. Epp, *Mennonite Exodus: The Rescue and Resettlement of the Russian Mennonites since the Communist Revolution* (Altona, MB: Canadian Mennonite Relief and Immigration Council, 1962), 231.

14   Erwin Warkentin, "The Mennonites before Moscow: The Notes of Dr. Otto Auhagen," *Journal of Mennonite Studies* 26 (2008): 205, 210.

15   Dyck, "Collectivization," 147.

16   Anna Janzen, letter fragment #1, 19 December 1929, OS; Anna Janzen, letter fragment #2, 20 February 1929, OS.

17   Dyck, "Collectivization," 149, 153.

18   Ibid., 149.

19   Ibid., 157–58.

20   Anna Janzen, letter fragment #1, 19 December 1929, OS. A verst is 1.067 kilometres.

21   Epp, *Mennonite Exodus,* 239.

22   Anna Janzen, letter fragment #1, 19 December 1929, OS.

23   Ibid.

24   John Werner, interview tape 1.

25   Anna Janzen, letter fragment #7, n.d.

26   Neil Sutherland, *Childhood in English Canada from the Great War to the Age of Television* (Toronto: University of Toronto Press, 1997), 12.

Chapter 3: Ivan, Stalin's Hope

1   Detlef Brandes and Andrej Savin, *Die Siberien-deutschen im Sovietstaat, 1919–1938* (Essen: Klartext, 2001), 314–15, 319–20.

2   Ibid., 337.

3   Ibid., 347.

4   Ibid., 353–55.

5   Anna Janzen, letter fragment #1, 19 December 1929, OS.

6   Orlando Figes, *The Whisperers: Private Life in Stalin's Russia* (New York: Henry Holt, 2007), xxx.

7   Anna Janzen, letter fragment #7, n.d.

8   Stalin, as quoted in Robert C. Tucker, *Stalin in Power: The Revolution from Above, 1928–1941* (New York: Norton, 1990), 46.

9   Anna Janzen, letter fragment #7, n.d. One *pud* is about sixteen kilograms.

10   Ibid.

11   Tucker, *Stalin in Power,* 190.

12   John Werner, interview tape 1, 22 March 1987.

13   Brandes and Savin, *Die Siberien-deutschen,* 387.

14   Anna Janzen, letter fragment #7, n.d.

15   As quoted in Figes, *The Whisperers,* 159.

16   Anna Janzen, letter fragment #6, 25 September 1934.

17   John Werner, interview tape 1, 22 March 1987.

18   Ibid.

19   Tucker, *Stalin in Power,* 321.

20   John Werner, interview tape 1, 22 March 1987. A *khutor* was a prosperous Ukrainian farm, and the term was adopted by Mennonites to designate a private estate owned by Mennonites outside the colony. There was a Wernersdorf in the Molotschna Mennonite Colony.

21 Ibid.

22 Figes, *The Whisperers,* 633.

23 John Werner, interview tape 1, 22 March 1987.

Chapter 4: The Mist Clears

1 Rennpenning was also a Siberian landowner. See Gerhard Fast, *In den Steppen Sibiriens* (Rosthern, SK: J. Heese, 1957), 139.

2 Tina Hinz, "Memoir," (Paderborn: n.p., 1968), 16.

3 Tina never mentioned the names of these villages. However, based on a brief family sketch by Katharina (Werner) Hamm, Jakob Werner, her grandfather, lived in the village of Skvortsovko (Skworzowo in German), approximately seventy kilometers from Petropavlovsk. Some families at a Werner event in Germany also suggested there was a Werner family in the village of Bulayewo, approximately twenty-five kilometers from Skvortsovka on the Trans-Siberian Railway. See "Werner-Harder Treffen," (Düren, Germany: n.p., 10 October 1992). Peter Rahn also mentions a J. Werner in Skvortsovka. See Peter Rahn, *Mennoniten in der Umgebung von Omsk* (Winnipeg: Christian Press, 1975), 126.

4 Hinz, "Memoir," 19.

5 One *desyatin* is 2.7 acres.

6 Fast, *In den Steppen Sibiriens,* 24.

7 Slavgorod was established in 1909 by the Russian government. Given that the family travelled in the spring of 1909, the town must have been just beginning.

8 Hinz, "Memoir," 27.

9 Ibid., 32; Fast, *In den Steppen Sibiriens,* 68.

10 Fast, *In den Steppen Sibiriens,* 93.

11 Jonathan D. Smele, *Civil War in Siberia: The Anti-Soviet Government of Admiral Kolchak 1918–1920* (Cambridge, UK: Cambridge University Press, 1996), Chapter 1.

12 Manfred Klaube, *Die Deutschen Dörfer in der Westsibirischen Kulunda-Steppe: Entwicklung, Strukturen, Probleme* (Marburg: N.G. Elwert Verlag, 1991), 42–43; Fast, *In den Steppen Sibiriens,* 96–97.

13 Hinz, "Memoir," 53.

14 Ibid., 54.

15 Tina suggested that two children of Johann and Anna (Janzen) Werner died in the epidemic, but there is no other evidence of this second child. In later letters to her daughter Aganetha in Canada, Anna referred only to an Anna who had died, and this reference is the only evidence she had been a victim of cholera.

16 Hinz, "Memoir," 55.

17 Jill Ker Conway, *When Memory Speaks: Exploring the Art of Autobiography* (Toronto: Random House, 1998), 16.

18 Hinz, "Memoir," 2, 132–33.

19   Andrew B. Stone, "'Overcoming Peasant Backwardness': The Khrushchev Anti-Religious Campaign and the Rural Soviet Union," *Russian Review* 67 (2008): 296–320. See also Walter Sawatzky, *Soviet Evangelicals since World War II* (Kitchener, ON: Herald Press, 1981), 131–56.

20   Hans Werner, "'German Only in Their Hearts': Making and Breaking the Ethnic German Diaspora in the 20th Century," in *Beyond the Nation?: Immigrants' Local Lives in Transnational Cultures*, ed. Alexander Freund (Toronto:University of Toronto Press, 2011), 211–226.

Chapter 5: War Stories

1   A report from a U.S. military attaché in Finland on 29 December 1939 noted "there are rumors that the new Russian divisions are made up largely of Caucasian and Siberian troops, believed to be of much higher quality than those already encountered." Frank B. Hayne, MA, Military Intelligence Reports, University of Winnipeg Archives, MFIL DK60.U16 1984, reel 10, frame 623.

2   John Werner, interview tape 3, 28 February 1988.

3   Alan F. Chew, *The White Death: The Epic of the Soviet–Finnish Winter War* (East Lansing, MI: Michigan State University Press, 1971), 149.

4   John Werner, interview tape 3, 28 February 1988.

5   Carl van Dyke, *The Soviet Invasion of Finland 1939–40* (London: Frank Cass, 1997), 152.

6   John Werner, interview tape 3, 28 February 1988.

7   John Werner, notes of a conversation, 18 January 1987.

8   Maksym Kolomyjec, *Tanks in the Winter War 1939–1940* (Stockholm: Leandoer and Ekholm Förlag, 2008), 93.

9   Cherkessians are a subgroup of the Circassian peoples who live in the Northern Caucasus area.

10   Donald Day's quotation in the *Chicago Tribune* appears frequently on websites on the theme of Jewish–Latvian relations. I have taken it from Frank Gordon, "Latvians and Jews between Germany and Russia," http://vip.latnet.lv/LPRA/fg_june.htm.

11   John Werner, interview tape 3, 28 February 1988.

12   Ibid.

13   Ibid.

14   David M. Glantz, ed., *The Initial Period of the War on the Eastern Front 22 June–August 1941* (London: Frank Cass, 1993), 187.

15   Tom Bergman, "Valerii Chkalov: Soviet Pilot as New Soviet Man," *Journal of Contemporary History* 33, 1 (1998): 138.

16   *Chkalov, Valery,* directed by Mikhail Kalatozov, starring V. Belokurov, S. Mezhinskii, and K. Tarasova, Lenfilm (black and white), 1941; see http://www.cohums.ohio-state.edu/slavicctr/filmsA-C.htm.

17   Alice M. Hoffman and Howard S. Hoffman, "Reliability and Validity in Oral History: The Case for Memory," in *Memory and History: Essays on Recalling and Interpreting Experience,* ed. Jaclyn Jeffrey and Glenace Edwall (Lanham, MD: University Press of America, 1994), 107–35. See also John E. Talbott, "Soldiers, Psychiatrists, and Combat Trauma," *Journal of Interdisciplinary History* 27, 3 (1997): 437–54.

18   Alice M. Hoffman and Howard S. Hoffman, *Archives of Memory: A Solder Recalls World War II* (Lexington: University Press of Kentucky, 1990), 87, 131.

Chapter 6: Johann: Becoming a German

1   John Erickson, *The Road to Stalingrad: Stalin's War with Germany,* vol. 1 (New York: Harper and Row, 1975), 98.

2   David M. Glantz, ed., "A Collection of Combat Documents Covering the First Three Days of the Great Patriotic War," *Journal of Slavic Military Studies* 4, 1 (1991): 165.

3   David M. Glantz, ed., *The Initial Period of the War on the Eastern Front 22 June–August 1941* (London: Frank Cass, 1993), 200–02.

4   John Werner, notes of a conversation, 6 January 2003. The 11th Mechanized Corps melted away; it lost all but 32 of its 305 tanks and after four days was left with 600 of its original 32,000-man complement. Robert Kirchubel, *Operation Barbarossa 1942 (3): Army Group Centre* (Oxford: Osprey, 2007), 37.

5   Stalin's Order No. 270, which required Red Army soldiers to commit suicide rather than be captured, was signed only in August 1941. Orlando Figes, *The Whisperers: Private Life in Stalin's Russia* (New York: Henry Holt, 2007), 411.

6   This is consistent with German Army policy regarding captured Red Army soldiers who were ethnic Germans. See, for instance, Ingeborg Fleischauer, *Das Dritte Reich und die Deutschen in der Sowjetunion* (Stuttgart: Deutsche Verlags-Anstalt, 1983), 87.

7   Alexander Dallin, *German Rule in Russia, 1941–45: A Study of Occupation Policies* (New York: Macmillan, 1957), 30–31.

8   John Werner, interview tape 3, 28 February 1988. It is not plausible that all *politruks* were Jews. Many Jews were attracted to the communist ideology and active in the Communist Party, and there were many Jewish *politruks*. The role of *politruk*, however, was not an ethnic or racial office, and it attracted other politically active communists.

9   Valdis O. Lumans, *Himmler's Auxiliaries: The Volksdeutsche Mittelstelle and National Minorities of Europe 1933–1945* (Chapel Hill: University of North Carolina Press, 1993), 161–72.

10   According to his application for citizenship, Ivan arrived in Pabianitz near Litzmannstadt (Łódź) in occupied Poland on 26 July 1941. This means the period of debriefing, interpreting, travelling, and imprisonment in Lublin was about one month. "Einburgerungsantrag," 6 October 1942, BDC.

11   John Werner, interview tape 3, 28 February 1988.

12 RKFDV is the acronym for the Reichskommisariat für die Festigung Deutschen Volkstums. See Robert L. Koehl, *RKFDV: German Resettlement and Population Policy 1939–1945* (Cambridge, MA: Harvard University Press, 1957), 104.

13 John Werner, interview tape 4, 23 March 1988.

14 Łódź fell to the Soviet forces on 19 January 1945.

15 EWZ 45, BDC, and "Führerschein" issued at Bamberg, 28 January 1947.

16 EWZ 3, EWZ 16, EWZ T/0114 , BDC. For documents without a title, I have chosen to refer to them by their form numbers, usually located in the bottom left-hand side of the form. See also Lumans, *Himmler's Auxiliaries*, 191; Koehl, *RKFDV,* 107.

Chapter 7: *The Fog of War*

1 Currently the Town of Ozersk, Province of Kalinograd, Russian Federation.

2 John Werner, interview tape 4, 23 March 1988.

3 Ibid.

4 John Werner, interview tape 5, 4 March 1988.

5 John Werner, interview tape 4, 23 March 1988.

6 John Werner, interview tape 6, summer 1988.

7 Stamm Batterie leichte Artillerie Ersatz Und Ausbildungs Abteilung (motorisiert) 103.

8 Paul E. Bauman, "Luftwaffe Airlift in the Tunisian Bridgehead: Expeditionary Lessons for a Transformation Age" (MA thesis, Maxwell Air Force Base, Alabama, School of Advanced Air and Space Studies, Air University, 2006), 69.

9 John Wheeler-Bennett, *The Nemesis of Power: The German Army in Politics 1918–1945* (London: Macmillan, 1953), 637–41, 678.

10 *The German Replacement Army (Ersatzheer)* (Washington, DC: Military Intelligence Division, 1944), 21–24.

11 Ulrich Neisser, "Memory with a Grain of Salt," in *Memory: An Anthology,* ed. Harriet Harvey Wood and A.S. Byatt (London: Vintage, 2009), 88.

12 Geoffrey Cubitt, *History and Memory* (Manchester: Manchester University Press, 2007), 76.

Chapter 8: *The 401*

1 John Werner, interview tape 6, summer 1988.

2 Ibid.

3 Units such as the 401 usually had some cannons of the 10 cm K 18 type, which had a maximum range of 19,075 metres. Ivan V. Hogg, *German Artillery of World War II* (London: Arms and Armour Press, 1975), 63.

4 John Werner, interview tape 5, 4 March 1988.

5   John Werner, interview tape 6, summer 1988. The reference to eight charges likely makes the cannon a 15 cm FH 18 model. Its range with the eighth charge, however, was 13,325 metres. Hogg, *German Artillery*, 63.

6   John Werner, interview tape 6, summer 1988. The reference to "Napolean Strasse" is unclear—a map by Richard Natkiel indicates a Napoleon route in the south of France (Nice–Grenoble), but this could not have been in that area. Richard Natkiel, *Atlas of World War II* (London: Bison Books, 1985), 176.

7   John Werner, interview tape 4, 23 March 1988.

8   John Werner, interview tape 6, summer 1988 and tape 4, 23 March 1988.

9   John Werner, interview tape 4, 23 March 1988.

10   Ibid.

11   John Werner, interview tape 6, summer 1988.

12   Ibid.

13   Ibid.

14   Bruce Quarrie, *The Ardennes Offensive: V Panzer Armee, Central Sector* (Oxford: Osprey, 2000), 13; "Lexikon der Wehrmacht," http://www.lexikon-der-wehrmacht.de/Gliederungen/VolksArtKorps/VolksArtKorps401.htm.

15   "Bundesarchiv to Dr. Horst Gerlach," 19 September 1989. The search for records in the German military archives was graciously assisted by Dr. Gerlach.

16   BundesArchiv (hereafter BA), RH 41/950, Part II, "Befehle-401, Abteilungsbefehl, Nr. 2," 3 October 1944.

17   BA, RH 41/950, Part I, "Befehle-401, Tagesbefehl," 2 November 1944.

18   BA, RH 41/949, "Kriegestagebuch Nr. 1," p. 2, 10 November 1944.

19   BA, 41/949, "Kriegestagebuch Nr. 1," pp. 9–11, 5–14 December 1944.

20   Charles B. Macdonald, *A Time for Trumpets: The Untold Story of the Battle of the Bulge* (New York: Bantam, 1985), 130.

21   BA, 41/949, "Kriegestagebuch Nr. 1," p. 11, 16 December 1944.

22   BA, 41/949, "Kriegestagebuch Nr. 1," p. 13, 19 December 1944.

23   Macdonald, *A Time for Trumpets*, 310.

24   BA, 41/949, "Kriegestagebuch Nr. 1," p. 21, 14 December 1944.

25   BA, RH 41/950, Part I, "Befehle-401, Tagesbefehl," 17 January 1945.

26   BA, RH 41/950, Part I, "Befehle-401, Tagesbefehl, Nr. 5," 18 January 1945.

27   BA, 41/948, "Kriegestagebuch Nr. 2," p. 2, 5–17 February 1945; RH 950, Part I, "Befehle-401, Tagesbefehl Nr. 8," 9 March 1945.

28   BA, 41/948, "Kriegestagebuch Nr. 2," pp. 2–3, 18 February–2 March 1945.

29   BA, 41/950, Part II, "Befehle—401, Abteilungsbefehl Nr. 22," 9 March 1945; 41/948, "Kriegestagebuch Nr. 2," p. 3, 8–11 March 1945.

30   Geoffrey Cubitt, *History and Memory* (Manchester: Manchester University Press, 2007), 130.

Chapter 9: The Collapse

1 BA, 41/948, "Kriegestagebuch Nr. 2," p. 3, 23 March 1945; Len Cacutt, ed., *Decisive Battles: The Turning Points of World War II* (New York: Gallery Books, 1986), 118.

2 John Werner, interview tape 6, summer 1988.

3 This might have been a result of the Germans opening the Schwammenaul Dam on 10 February 1945 to slow the advance of the Americans.

4 John Werner, interview tape 4, 23 March 1988.

5 John Werner, interview tape 6, summer 1988. The soldier's quip did not come up in the formal interviews, but was an often repeated feature of my father's stories.

6 John Werner, interview tape 4, 23 March 1988; Deutsche Dienstelle, VI/313, 20.10.1988.

7 Frank Kermode, "Palaces of Memory," in *Memory: An Anthology*, ed. Harriet Harvey Wood and A.S. Byatt (London: Vintage, 2009), 9.

8 John Werner, interview tape 4, 23 March 1988.

9 John Werner, notes of a conversation, 15 October 1989.

10 John Werner, interview tape 4, 23 March 1988.

11 James Bacque, *Other Losses* (Toronto: Stoddart, 1989).

12 Steven Ambrose, "Ike and the Disappearing Atrocities," *New York Times Book Review*, 24 February 1991, http://www.nytimes.com/books/98/11/22/specials/ambrose-atrocities.html.

13 Robert S. Anderson, ed., *Preventative Medicine in World War II, Volume IX, Special Fields* (Washington, DC: United States Army, 1969), 378–79; Bacque, *Other Losses*, 22–23.

14 John Werner, interview tape 5, 4 March 1988.

15 John Werner, interview tape 4, 23 March 1988.

16 John Werner, notes of a conversation, 15 October 1989.

17 John Werner, interview tape 4, 23 March 1988.

18 John Werner, interview tape 5, 4 March 1988.

19 Ibid.

20 Ibid.

Chapter 10: New Beginnings

1 John Werner, interview tape 5, 4 March 1988. My father had a "Prisoner of War Discharge" document dated 21 August 1946 at Regensburg. It was signed by Fred E. Wilson and has a stamp with "1st Infantry Division Discharge Center" on it. The same date is noted in the transcript of his military record. Deutsche Dienstelle, VI/313, 20.10.1988.

2 David Thelen, "An Afterthought on Scale and History," *Journal of American History* 77, 2 (1990): 591.

3 John Werner, interview tape 5, 4 March 1988. My father had a letter from the Civilian Labor Office of the 3492nd Ordnance MAM Company dated 17 January 1947 certifying his employment with the above from 28 August 1946 to 17 January 1947. There is also a document from the Nurnberg Military Post APO 139 US Army, Bamberg Sub-Post, dated 31 May 1949, certifying his employment from 17 January 1947 to 31 January 1949 and again from 10 February 1949 to 23 March 1949.

4 On another occasion, he remembered him as Buhler. John Werner, notes of a conversation, 14 September 1986.

5 One of my father's documents from these years is an employee's pass for the "Artillery Kaserne," indicating that my father was a driver for the BMSP (Bamberg Military Sub-Post) Motor Pool.

6 Goering began his testimony on 13 March 1946 and along with the other defendants made his final statement on 31 August 1946. Goering died on 15 October by poisoning himself by taking a cyanide pill smuggled into his cell. In his final statement, written as a suicide note, Goering appealed to the tribunal to be shot as a soldier rather than being hanged. I found no evidence that Goering made this statement in the courtroom, where my father could have heard it. He did indicate this in a letter to his wife Emily. See G.M. Gilbert, Nuremburg Diary (New York: Farrar, Strauss, 1947), 194–216, and Ben E. Swearingen, The Mystery of Hermann Goering's Suicide (London: Robert Hale, 1990), 43–59.

7 John Werner, interview tape 5, 4 March 1988.

8 MHC, CMBC, vol. 1331, file 993.

9 Motor Pool, Nurnberg Military Post, Bamberg Sub-Post, APO 139, U.S. Army, "Bestaetigung," 31 May 1949.

10 In his taped interview, he mentioned Ludwigsburg; in documents of the day, he indicated he was processed at Nellingen, the IRO's Area 2 headquarters.

11 Marie K. Wiens, "Activity Report, January, February, March, Fallingbostel, Germany," Mennonite Church Archives (hereafter MCA), Goshen, IN, IX-19-9, box 1, file 1/75, C.F. Klassen files—Refugee Migration, Fallingbostel, 1949–50, MCC Europe and North Africa Collection.

12 O. Cormier, "Memorandum: Re: Johann Werner, German Ser. No. 31621," 8 June 1949, MCA, IX-19-16, box 13, file 2, Refugee Personnel Files, Wei.–Wer., MCC Europe and North Africa Collection.

13 David J. Quapp to Siegfried Janzen, 5 July 1949, and J.H.W. Hudson, IRO, to MCC, 5 July 1949, MCA, IX-19-16, box 10, file 10/11, IRO Reports on Immigration, 1948–52, MCC Europe and North America Refugee Materials.

14 "Allgemeinen MCC Fragebogen," 25 April 1949, MCA, IX-19-16, box 7, file 4, Refugee Personnel Questionnaires, We-Wiebe, H., MCC Europe and North Africa Collection.

15 Undated statement, MCA, IX-19-16, box 13, file 2, Refugee Personnel Files, Wei.–Wer., MCC Europe and North Africa Collection.

16 Ted Regehr, "Of Dutch or German Ancestry? Mennonite Refugees, MCC, and the International Refugee Organization," *Journal of Mennonite Studies* 13 (1995): 19.

17 Siegfried Janzen to Frank Wiens, 29 April 1949, MCA, IX-14-2, box 2, MCC Gronau Files—Corres. Fallingbostel A–L, file 25, General Correspondence, MCC Europe and North Africa Collection.

18 Louise W. Holborn, *The International Refugee Organization: A Specialized Agency of the United Nations, Its History and Work, 1946–1952* (London: Oxford University Press, 1956), 586; Frank H. Epp, *Mennonite Exodus: The Rescue and Resettlement of the Russian Mennonites since the Communist Revolution* (Altona, MB: Canadian Mennonite Relief and Immigration Council, 1962), 405–06.

19 S. Scheuring, Regional Eligibility Officer, to S. Janzen, MCC, 21 September 1949, MCA, IX-19-16, box 13, file 2, Refugee Personnel Files, Wei.–Wer., MCC Europe and North Africa Collection.

20 John Werner, notes of a conversation, 14 September 1986.

21 Ibid.

22 Personal document, "Abkehr-Schein, 24.6.1952," Eisen und Hüttenwerke, Lohnbuchhaltung.

23 G.R. Gaeddert to Johann Werner, 14 November 1950 and 26 February 1951; Margarete Vogt to G.R. Gaeddert, 23 August 1951, MCA, IX-19-16, box 13, file 2, Refugee Personnel Files, Wei.–Wer., MCC Europe and North Africa Collection.

Chapter 11: Margarethe (Sara) Vogt (Letkeman)

1 Margaret Werner, interview tape 2, summer 1987.

2 Ibid.

3 Ibid.

4 Ibid.

5 Ibid.

6 "Osterwick Village Report: List of 213 abducted persons," www.mennonite genealogy.com/russia/jr/ostabd.htm. This list is transcribed and translated from reports created for the Minister of Occupied Eastern Territories between 1941 and 1944, which are part of the Captured German Documents located in the Library of Congress. The reports for the village of Osterwick are in: box 6, reels 2-3, German Captured Documents Collection, Manuscript Division, Library of Congress, Washington, D.C.

7 Margaret Werner, interview, tape 2, summer 1987.

8 Ibid.

9 Steve J. Stern, *Remembering Pinochet's Chile: On the Eve of London, 1998* (Durham: Duke University Press, 2006), 7–8, 116.

10 It seems my mother did not know about this event first-hand, which apparently became part of the villagers' collective memory. The story of the Lutheran pastor–soldier is also told in J.J. Neudorf, D.H. Rempel, and H.J. Neudorf, eds., *Osterwick, 1812–1943* (Clearbrook, BC: A. Olfert, 1973), 176.

11 Margaret Werner, interview tape 7, 28 January 1989.

12 "Allgemeinen MCC Fragebogen," 27 March 1949, MCA, IX-19-16, box 7, file 2, Refugee Personnel Questionnaires, V, MCC Europe and North Africa Collection.

13 Margaret Werner, interview tape 7, 28 January 1989. My mother's account might refer to what Gerhard Rempel calls the "Massacre at Zaporozhia." See Gerhard Rempel, "Mennonites and the Holocaust: From Collaboration to Perpetuation," *Mennonite Quarterly Review* 84 (2010): 507–50.

14 Margaret Werner, interview tape 7, 28 January 1989.

15 Neudorf, Rempel, and Neudorf, *Osterwick,* 157; "Einbürgerungsantrag," 14 May 1944, BDC.

16 My mother suggested he had been drafted, though few Mennonites were drafted into the German Army before they arrived in the Warthegau in 1943.

17 Margaret Werner, interview tape 7, 28 January 1989.

18 "Abschrift der Einburgerungsurkunde," 14 April 1944, BDC.

19 The Soviet offensive would be diverted, and Ratibor would be captured only on 31 March 1945.

20 Margaret Werner, interview tape 7, 28 January 1989.

21 An account by Helena Wiens in the German-language newspaper *Der Bote* suggests they arrived in Wernigerode on 9 or 10 February. In her account, the train route was Opava–Olomouc–Prague–Dresden–Halle–Wernigerode. Helena Wiens, "Die Erinnerungen eines 17 jährigen Mädchens aus dem Jahre 1945," *Der Bote,* 19 April 1989, 8.

22 Margaret Werner, interview tape 7, 28 January 1989. My mother's recollection of the date was 5 May 1945; however, the account by Wiens puts the date at 11 April. The latter date coincides more accurately with maps of the front at the time. See Richard Natkiel, *Atlas of World War II* (London: Bison Books, 1985), 187.

23 Margaret Werner, interview tape 7, 28 January 1989.

24 "Resettlement Medical Examination Forms," MCA, IX-19-6, box 8/6, file L, MCC Europe and North Africa Collection.

Chapter 12: *The Immigrants*

1 MCC Hard Core Record, Case No. MCC/38-B, MCA, IX-19-16, box 8/6, Resettlement Medical Examination Forms, MCC, North Africa and Europe Refugee Materials.

2 P.W. Bird, CGIM, to MCC, 21 September 1949, MCA, IX-19-16, box 12/38, Refugee Personnel Files, Vogt, A.-S., MCC, North Africa and Europe Refugee Materials.

3 Margarethe Werner to Regier, 25 February 1952, MCA, IX-19-16, box13/2, Refugee Personnel Files, Wei.-Wer.; G.R. Gaeddert to Margaret Vogt, 13 January 1951, MCA, IX-19-16, box 7/35, Refugee Personnel Files, Let.-Lic.

4 Margarethe Vogt to G.R. Gaeddert, 23 August 1951, MCA, IX-19-16, box 13/2, Refugee Personnel Files, Wei.-Wer., MCC, North Africa and Europe Refugee Materials.

5   C.F. Klassen to P.W. Bird, 7 April 1952, MCA, IX-19-9, C.F. Klassen Files, Canadian Government Immigration Mission, 1947–53.

6   Anne Giesbrecht to Elma Esau, 14 May 1952, MCA, IX-19-16, box 9, CMBC, 1949–55, MCC, North Africa and Europe Refugee Materials.

7   Margarethe Werner to Frieda Dirksen, 20 June 1952, MCA, IX-19-16, box 13/2, Refugee Personnel Files, Wei.-Wer., MCC, North Africa and Europe Refugee Materials.

8   Anne Giesbrecht to J.J. Thiessen, 26 June 1952, MHC, CMBC, vol. 1364.

9   Personal document, "Abkehr-Schein, 24.6.1952," Eisen und Hüttenwerke, Lohnbuchhaltung and "Immigration Card," MCA, IX-19-16, box 13/2, Refugee Personnel Files, Wei.-Wer., North Africa and Europe Refugee Materials.

10   Notes of a conversation with Margaret Werner, 6 February 2010.

11   http://www.theshipslist.com/ships/descriptions/ShipsB.html.

12   J. Gerbrandt to John Werner, 30 April 1953, and Katharina Vogt to CMBC Board, 12 April 1952, MHC, CMBC, vol. 1364, file 1317.

13   "Saskatchewan Mennonite Cemetery Finding Aid," Mennonite Historical Society of Saskatchewan, Drake Cemetery, Margaret Ewert, 8 March 2006, and "Mennonite Central Committee, Hard Core Record," MHC, CMBC, vol. 1364, file 1317.

14   In another conversation, he remembered it being $150 per month. John Werner, notes of a conversation, 14 September 1986.

Chapter 13: Memories, Stories, and History

1   Manfred Klaube, *Die Deutschen Dörfer in der Westsibirischen Kulunda-Steppe: Entwicklung, Strukturen, Probleme* (Marburg: N.G. Elwert Verlag, 1991), 91.

2   Linda Vogt to Erwin Vogt and Marie Rempel, 5 April 1967. The letter is in the possession of Edna Vogt.

3   Alice M. Hoffman and Howard S. Hoffman, *Archives of Memory: A Solder Recalls World War II* (Lexington: University Press of Kentucky, 1990), 145.

4   Richard F. Thompson and Stephen A. Madigan, *Memory: The Key to Consciousness* (Washington, DC: Joseph Henry Press, 2005), 181; Ulrich Neisser, "Memory with a Grain of Salt," in *Memory: An Anthology*, ed. Harriet Harvey Wood and A.S. Byatt (London: Vintage, 2009), 82.

5   Susan Engel, *Context Is Everything: The Nature of Memory* (New York: Freeman, 1999), 15.

6   Hoffman and Hoffman, *Archives of Memory*, 148.

7   Engel, *Context Is Everything*, 147.

8   Augustine, *Confessions*, as quoted in Frank Kermode, "Palaces of Memory," in *Memory: An Anthology*, ed. Harriet Harvey Wood and A.S. Byatt (London: Vintage, 2009), 3–4.

9   Neisser, "Memory with a Grain of Salt," 81.

10 Geoffrey Cubitt, *History and Memory* (Manchester: Manchester University Press, 2007), 76.

11 Steven Rose, "'Memories Are Made of This,'" in *Memory: An Anthology,* edited by Harriet Harvey Wood and A.S. Byatt (London: Vintage Books, 2009), 65. See also Cubitt, *History and Memory,* 77.

12 Cyril Connolly, *The Unquiet Grave* (1944), as quoted in Harriet Harvey Wood and A.S. Byatt, eds., *Memory: An Anthology* (London: Vintage, 2009), 398.

13 Cubitt, *History and Memory,* 76.

14 Jill Ker Conway, *When Memory Speaks: Exploring the Art of Autobiography* (Toronto: Random House, 1998), 7.

15 Ibid., 14.

16 Ibid., 11–12.

17 Marlene Epp, *Women without Men: Mennonite Refugees of the Second World War* (Toronto: University of Toronto Press, 2000), 15, 12.

18 David Thelen, "An Afterthought on Scale and History," *Journal of American History* 77, 2 (1990): 591.

19 Roger Horowitz, "Oral History and the Story of America and World War II," *Journal of American History* 82, 2 (1995): 618.

20 Ibid., 619.

21 Cubitt, *History and Memory,* 36.

22 Marina Lewycka, *A Short History of Tractors in Ukrainian* (New York: Penguin, 2005), 249.

Index